more...

thin threads

Life Changing Moments

Real Stories
of Life Changing Moments

COMPILED BY

Stacey K. Battat

kiwi·publishing

Woodbridge, Connecticut

Thin Thread® More Real Stories of Life Changing Moments

Published by: Kiwi Publishing, Inc.
Post Office Box 3852
Woodbridge CT 06525
info@kiwipublishing.com
www.kiwipublishing.com
203-295-0370

ISBN 978-1-935-768-05-0
UPC # 1396428768
First Edition: November, 2010

Dedication

I DEDICATE THIS BOOK to my life partner, husband and love of my life. Thank you for holding my hand on the wildest ride of all... our life, and for giving me the freedom to wander and discover my very own "beaches."

thin threads \thĭn thrĕdz\ *n* :

    moments, events, setbacks, crossroads or encounters that connect us to a person, place or opportunity and change our lives for the better

Contents

Introduction

I F YOU CALL my home looking for me a common response from anyone answering is: "She's taking a walk." Walking has always been the most grounding activity in my life. Each step I take offers me tremendous balance, whether I am strengthening myself through exercise, or feeling fragile and "hanging on by a thin thread."

The cover of the first *Thin Threads Anthology* depicts two paths through the woods. Now, for our latest anthology, I've chosen an image that shows small steps in the sand, because I truly believe that we find our most wondrous openings in the small steps we take.

We named the series *Thin Threads* because the true magic happens in the sometimes veiled threads that connect us as we take these small steps during our journey. Whether we are connecting to nature or to a stranger, finding new inspiration in old relationships or feeling humbled in the face of this ominous universe or connections to a higher power, these openings are what make life worth living.

Often when thoughts are crowding my mind, walking helps me to slow down and become fully aware of my five senses and what they are experiencing. When I walk, I often reflect and become thankful for the people and places that have brought me to this moment in my journey. This is when my mind is at its quietest and the "connecting thoughts" appear that I know I must truly listen! In this way, I continue to experience "thin thread" connections that offer up new possibilities, new paths, new friendships and a plethora of "new" to learn and experience in this world!

At one point in my wanderings, I repeatedly envisioned the image of a woman I had met only once as a workshop leader. About 20 years ago, I was working toward my counseling degree and took a graduate institute workshop entitled *Healing, Education, Laughter and Play.* It was led by Joyce Saltman, a professor of special education. Joyce was the first inspirational speaker I had ever heard, and she appeared bigger than life to me.

I decided to act on whim and looked her up. I didn't know WHY I was calling, and told her so, but I also told her that I had begun collecting *"thin thread"* stories for a book series, and that I hoped we could meet again in person. She was struck by the name of our company and said that she would be happy to get together. Within months of our first meeting, Joyce became not only my mentor and a partner in our business, but also one of my closest friends. Together we released *Thin Threads of Teachers & Mentors.* We have all experienced crossroads, including both progress and setbacks, where we usually have a choice to make. Perhaps doors have opened in your life and have led you down an unexpected pathway to a new beginning. Perhaps you found yourself in a strange place or had a fateful interaction with a stranger. Each of us has these "thin thread" moments – moments when a decision we made, or even a small detour we took in our lives, laid before us a new path. If we recognize these moments, particularly when life hands us lemons, we open ourselves to potentially life-altering new paths, and support one another in the universe.

Stacey Battat, Editor-in-Chief

More Thin Threads

Frosty

Crossing the right road can change your life

Madeleine Kuderick

M Y FAMILY HAD just moved to Oak Park and, as a shy
seven year old, I dreaded being the new kid at Hatch
Elementary School. My stomach twisted in knots as I trudged
down the block, past the big, blue mailbox, and over to the
busy intersection at Ridgeland Avenue. The brick school
building loomed across the street and I could hear the shouts
of gigantic sixth graders on the playground, probably waiting
to trample me. I wanted to turn around and run back home.
But then I saw Frosty.

I'd never seen a crossing guard before. Not up close anyway.
But there she was, walking across the street, bending down
to shake my hand. When she leaned in, I could see the blue
sparkle of her eyes and smell the powdery scent of skin cream
on her cheeks.

"Everybody calls me Frosty," she said. Then she gave my
hand a little squeeze. "You'll do just great today!"

I don't know why, but somehow I believed her.

A smile spread across Frosty's face and the wrinkles around
her eyes deepened. She pulled a peppermint from her pocket
and slipped it into my hand.

2

"I'll have another piece of candy waiting for you after school," she promised. "Then you can tell me all about your day."

I stood on the corner as Frosty marched back to the middle of the busy intersection and stretched her arms out wide. She looked strong and important wearing her dark blue uniform with silver buttons and bright, white gloves. The cars slowed to a stop and Frosty ushered me safely across the street.

I don't remember anything else about my first day at Hatch Elementary School. But I do remember meeting Frosty.

As time went on, I began to look forward to those comings and goings across Ridgeland Avenue. Don't get me wrong. I never really got over being the new kid at school and spent most of my elementary years as the last student picked for Phys. Ed. teams and the first one to be teased. Still, I always felt a rush of excitement when the school bell rang. I'd run to the mulberry tree at the end of the playground and wait until the other kids crossed the street. Then, when I had Frosty all to myself, I'd tell her how I got an A minus on my spelling test or that I won a goldfish at the church carnival. Sometimes, I'd slip a poem in her pocket, something I'd written just for her. Frosty would pat the paper inside her uniform and tell me how she'd treasure my words.

"I know you're going to be a writer one day," Frosty assured me.

And somehow, I believed her.

Over time, I came to rely on those moments and the comfort of our routine: peppermints on Mondays; butterscotch on Wednesdays; a stick of gum on Fridays when I walked an extra block to my friend's house after school. Frosty said gum lasted longer than candy and I could blow bubbles the whole way there. She remembered my birthdays with a shiny silver dollar, and she knew when I made my first communion or when I lost a tooth. I'm sure Frosty must've felt sick some days, or dreaded standing in the freezing winter wind. But for all the years I attended Hatch Elementary School, I don't remember her ever missing a single day of crossing guard duty.

It's amazing to think what an impact she could make in the 15 steps it took to cross Ridgeland Avenue. No matter what happened, I knew Frosty would listen to my every word like there was nothing more important than hearing how my hamster got stuck in its Habitrail or how I failed my multiplication tables for the eighth time. Frosty always knew just what to say. By the time I reached the other side of the street, my spirit felt lighter and I believed in myself again, even in my dreams to write.

Of course, I knew deep down that Frosty gave the same kind of guidance and encouragement to all the other kids, especially the ones who walked out of their way just to cross at Frosty's intersection. She held her post for nearly 30 years and sometimes I'd see the older kids return with a report card in hand, or a shiny class ring, or even a letterman jacket. They'd wait on the corner, anxious to show Frosty their latest accomplishments, beaming like they were still seven years old. I didn't know it then, but one day I'd return to that same corner myself, at 17, proud to tell Frosty how I'd been elected editor-in-chief of the high school newspaper. Just like she knew I would.

It's been almost 40 years since Frosty first walked me across Ridgeland Avenue. I'm not a shy school girl any longer. In fact, I've grown to achieve much success in my professional career and in my writing pursuits. Still, I have to wonder how much of this I owe to Frosty and to the encouragement she gave me at a fragile time when I needed it the most.

I never knew Frosty's real name. I never saw the color of her hair beneath her uniform cap. In fact, I never spent more than a few minutes crossing the road with her each day. Yet somehow, in the brevity of those moments, Frosty left a memory so enduring I cannot think of her today without feeling a lump in my throat. I can see her still: arms outstretched, eyes smiling, white gloves waving me across the road.

I'm sure Frosty knew back then what I am only now discovering; that even in the slightest intersection of lives, there lies an opportunity to make a powerful difference — to listen, to love and to change someone forever.

Winner of the Thin Threads contest for best story in 2010

Vancouver & My Dad

A lick goodbye

Mary Johnson

I T HAS BEEN said that when our loved ones die they never leave. Instead, they remain with us in some mystical and special way. My dad's death from brain cancer in 2001 put this theory to the test.

My dad instilled in me a desire to write stories and a love for dogs. He encouraged me to write stories and I would read them to him over the phone. His critiques were honest and we treasured those conversations. My dad and mom owned many dogs in his lifetime but this story focuses on his last dog, Vancouver. Vancouver was a big yellow Lab who was named for the place where my parents purchased him as a puppy from a Canadian breeder.

My parents lavished love and affection on that dog and my dad continued a tradition he had established with his previous dogs. He chose a brown leather collar and leash and would replace them when the leather became frayed or worn.

Dad walked his dog every day. Vancouver obeyed him without question and they made a handsome sight. During my visits home, he taught me the proper way to hold a leash. I still use the technique with my dogs today.

My dad endowed Vancouver with human qualities. My father would sit at the piano, play some notes, and telephone my girls, who were then very young, to tell them that Vancouver was practicing and that he was one of few dogs that could play the piano. The girls loved this story and he repeated it often.

Vancouver was a constant part of his life, from his waking up to the end of his day. If he sat down to read, which he did a lot, Vancouver could be found either directly on his lap or at his feet. Visitors would have to tell Vancouver how wonderful he was as they entered the house. My dad's exact words were, "Have you told Vancouver how handsome he is today?"

My dad was diagnosed with brain cancer in June of 1999 and his struggle ended in February of 2001. During that time, he took care of Vancouver as long as his body would allow him to. On one of my visits, I remember observing my dad and his dog walking with my girls during the big leaf season (fall) in Washington State. He watched my girls take turns holding Vancouver's leash and I could see a big smile on his face.

I visited my dad when I could so that my girls would not forget him. My parents lived in a two-story home and he had great difficulty walking up and down the stairs. Vancouver would wait for him to come down the stairs every morning and not budge until he was safely downstairs. Vancouver was in for a long wait as my dad needed lots of time to make it to the first floor.

One of the few laughs of that heartbreaking trip was the trouble that Vancouver and my dog, Woody, got into when no one was looking. I had driven up from Los Angeles with my girls and Woody for a week-long visit. One evening my dad carried a 20-pound bag of dog food to the porch and left it there. In the morning, we let the dogs out to do their "thing" and we did not hear from them for a long time. We stepped outside after our breakfast and discovered that Vancouver and Woody had opened the bag together and consumed 99 percent of the dog food. Both of the dogs looked pregnant and could not move for three days.

Brain cancer took its toll and my dad was dying. He could not walk anymore and his ability to talk was gone. I took up my girls to say their goodbyes to him. Hospice was easing him to his inevitable death as he lay in a bed in the downstairs den. I stayed up with him every night, administered morphine and monitored him for signs of distress or pain. He communicated with his eyes, which told us anything we needed to know. The girls and their cousins played with Vancouver but the family focused all of its attention on my dad. He lingered on death's door but he was not ready to go yet. What was he missing?

I discovered the answer to this question as I read a book on dying that was given to us by hospice. Trust me to say this reading was difficult but I did it anyway. The book stated that people who are dying need to say goodbye to those people and things that made their life complete and special. My dad had said goodbye to his family but he still needed to say goodbye to something else.

I had an idea. I asked my mom if Dad had seen Vancouver since he had become bedridden. She said that my dad had not seen Vancouver for several weeks. In fact, Vancouver had been the least of her concerns during these last painful weeks. I told her to bring Vancouver to the den and helped him jump onto the bed. Vancouver immediately lay his head on my dad's stomach. My dad opened his eyes and stroked his dog's head. Tears streamed down his face and his eyes smiled. It may have been my imagination but I know that Vancouver was crying as well.

My dad died that very night and it is my honest belief that saying goodbye to his dog gave him the peace and closure to leave this earth and go to heaven.

As for me, I now have two dogs that have leather collars and every morning I tell them how wonderful they are. By writing this story of my dad's journey with Vancouver and continuing his tradition of loving dogs in my own life, my dad remains with me in a mystical and special way.

Polka Dots & Sunshine Teardrops

A new view from The Magic Kingdom

Jim Fox

THERE HAVE BEEN ROLLER COASTER highs and lows in my life, exhilarating successes and soul-numbing defeats. There are also cherished moments of the best life can offer: my wedding day, the births of our two sons, the adoption of our daughter, and the day that mouse in polka dots squeezed my arm.

I keep these cherished moments deep inside because I'm not an emotional guy. Oh, I can rage over injustices, but true to my gender, I remain stoic in the face of small joys and even miraculous events— like that day with the mouse. However, I've often been chided by Marsha, my wife, for wearing depression like a heavy smothering cape. That's because she refuses to accept just how unfair life can be. She has faith that bad times fade and life always gets better. But it was that mouse in polka dots that taught me there are many others who share her optimism.

Several years ago, I returned to California to seek employment. The job I landed didn't offer much potential and my ego was bruised by this not-so-fruitful job search. It didn't help that although we were on a tight budget, friends and relatives insisted that we couldn't come back to California and not take our boys to Disneyland. Somehow, this notion was implanted in the boy's heads, so when summer arrived they made great plans about what to do at Disneyland.

Facing the inevitable, we set out in the wee hours of the morning, with the boys asleep in the car, arriving at Disneyland as the gates opened. Once inside the park, our boys, armed with "mad money" from grandma, decided they had to buy something in one of the shops on Main Street. I am not a shopper, so I stayed outside leaning against a lamppost. I was fatigued from the long drive and had a sour stomach from too much coffee. In this blue mood, I surveyed the street. A teenaged staff member in a striped vest and straw hat quickly swept up a paper wrapper carelessly discarded a moment earlier. Across the street, a perky woman at a vendor's cart cheerfully gave a balloon to a tyke riding on an adult's shoulders. "Minimum wage summer help," I grumbled cynically, settling deeper into my blue mood. "Bet they can't keep smiling all day."

I listened to the voices of people gathered at the small tables nearby, enjoying breakfast from the shop next door. I turned to see who was speaking in a melodious Caribbean accent. A tall black man, in a Panama hat and an outrageously colorful Calypso shirt, was laughing with a friend. At the next table sat a middle-aged woman with raven black hair pulled tightly into a bun, looking overdressed in her European-cut pantsuit. "She's Spanish or Portuguese," I thought. Then an odd contraption at the next table caught my eye and a chill swept over me. In a walker, a large steel oval on casters, a young boy swayed precariously in a harness suspended from a cable. I realized as he struggled towards his mother that the boy was afflicted with cerebral palsy, and the walker gave him mobility. His father snapped a picture with a camera and both parents were enjoying the glee with which their son was taking in the sites of The Magic Kingdom. A feeling of shame crept over me. I'd been wallowing in a sullen mood of self-pity, yet I had two healthy boys who were just as gleeful about their visit to Disneyland.

My somber reflection was interrupted by a commotion in the street. Children were shouting and laughing where, as if by magic, Disney characters had appeared on the sidewalk. Clumsy Goofy stumbled through the crowd while Pluto the Dog trotted along leading a parade of kids. I took my camera bag off my shoulder, sure that my boys would rush out of the souvenir shop. A squeal of joy erupted behind me and, turning, I saw the little boy in the walker struggling towards me, an autograph book clutched in his hands, but his delighted gaze obviously wasn't meant for me. I turned to find myself face to face with a very large mouse head topped by a huge polka dot bow. Back at the tables, Calypso Man laughed and shouted, "It's de mouse! It's de mouse!" The kid inside the polka dot skirt and Minnie Mouse head made an appreciative curtsy. The crowd clapped and cheered, and I smiled.

The blues were just beginning to slip away when I heard a murmur of concern from the crowd. Turning, I could see the child in the walker faltering as the caster wheels caught in the cracks between the bricks of the little dining patio. He was struggling towards Minnie Mouse, but there were still several tables around which he had to navigate. Goofy and Pluto were moving on down the sidewalk, and alongside me, Minnie was signing the last autograph book held out by an admirer.

A dark feeling descended upon me, as if I were standing in the eye of a storm about to sweep over me with suffocating depression. How could life be this unfair? In desperation, I spoke to the mouse character. "Minnie, there's a little boy who wants to see you!" I pointed over my shoulder. Minnie Mouse gazed at the boy and then at the other characters moving down the street. The mouse again turned toward the little boy, and I realized the kid inside the costume was in a quandary about whether to follow the park rules and keep moving through the crowd or to wait a few minutes more for one solitary child. Then the big rubber nose pushed towards me, and a gloved hand reached over and squeezed my arm—hard. My heart seemed to skip a beat as understanding flowed through me. "I think Minnie is going to wait," I cried out. Minnie squeezed my arm again and made a thumbs-up gesture.

As realization swept through the breakfast crowd, there was a flurry of activity among these total strangers. Calypso Man jumped up and grabbed the corner of his table. "Quick! We con move de tables, Mon," he shouted to his friend. The Portuguese Lady stood and snatched up the breakfast trays, moving them quickly out of the way. There was the scrape of metal and the scuffle of feet as tables were moved to create a pathway for the child in his walker. One more obstacle remained; a small hedge with a miniature wrought iron fence stood between the mouse and the boy. Grabbing my arm for support, Minnie leaned far over and tousled the boy's hair as he struggled into reach. Minnie accepted his autograph book and signed it with a flourish. As she handed the book back and squeezed the boy's shoulder in a one-handed hug, he shrieked in delight and turned towards his parents, a gigantic smile on his face. Minnie gave a quick wave and skipped off, leaving a delighted child and two parents with tears welling up in their eyes. The little boy, chortling in delight, thrust the book at his mother who swept him into her arms. "Yes, it was Minnie," she chanted, as proud pappa kept snapping photos. "Yes, it was Minnie! Minnie Mouse!"

The Portuguese Lady was blubbering into her handkerchief. As Calypso Man turned to replace the moved tables, he and I made eye contact. There were tears in his eyes too.

Wiping his cheek, he chuckled and said, "Mon, it's de sun! Too bright!" Laughing, he held out his wet palm, "See, sunshine tear drops!" Dabbing my own cheeks with my T-shirt sleeve, I grinned back at him and said, "Yeah, sunshine and L.A. smog!" Calypso Man winked, nodded his head, and then with the look of a very wise sage, said, "Still, it's a good day." I thought about the small miracle that had just occurred among so many strangers. "A good day," I repeated. "A really good day." Glancing around, I realized my boys had run off after Minnie Mouse, with Marsha in close pursuit. "I've got to go," I stammered awkwardly. "My kids…" Calypso Man shrugged and making an impatient shoving gesture, he cried, "Go, Mon!" As I turned to sprint after my family, he called out, "Got to love de Mouse!" Slinging my camera bag over one shoulder, I pumped my fist skyward and shouted back, "Got to love this place!" Running down the street, oblivious

to the people around me, I thrust my fists skyward and joy-
fully shouted, "It is a really good day!"

Through the years, I've had occasion to recall that day
and sometimes to tell someone of that small miracle. And,
although I am not an emotional guy, I have to blink away
those sunshine tears. It is then I find myself subconsciously
rubbing my arm where that squeeze from some kid in a sum-
mertime job reawakened hope and joy within me.

Winner of the Thin Threads contest for best story in 2009

Thank You Grandma Tillie

Legacies are priceless

Howard Gleichenhaus

T HE ROOM IS small and cold, the furniture hard and institutional. Cheap oil-painting reproductions hang askew on a far wall. Aunt Dorothy sits across from me, her face buried in a tissue. She weeps softly. The door opens and my mother comes in, her eyes are red and swollen. She points toward a long hallway.

Following three painted stripes on the gray tile floor, I walk with trepidation. The blue stripe continues down as far as I can see, the yellow makes a right turn at an intersecting corridor and the red one goes left. I follow the red one until in front of me are two large swinging doors with square windows. Above in bold black letters are the words, INTENSIVE CARE.

Inside I hear machines beeping and clicking. Monitors with jagged lines, moving across green screens, are keeping vigil on critically ill patients. Silently, floating past me as if on cushions of air, nurses in starched white uniforms with pointy caps and gold pins drift from bed to bed. They all look so serious.

In the far corner of the room, I catch my first glimpse of Grandma Tillie. She looks small in the large bed. Her eyes are not open, nor are they closed. Her hair, completely white, is spread across a pillow and someone has put rouge on her cheeks. There is too much, I think. She looks like a child's doll. Her lips are pale, almost blue, and her breathing is labored but even. For several seconds I stand and watch her chest rise and fall beneath the pale blue blanket. A pink satin bed-jacket peeks out from beneath her covers. There is a chair near the bed. I pull it close, sit and gently grasp her hand. It feels cold. I squeeze her thin fingers and caress the gold wedding band that Grandpa Harry placed on her hand so long ago. For several minutes, I gaze at her beautiful face.

Grandma Tillie left Europe with a few cherished possessions to remind her of loved ones and crossed a vast ocean in search a better life. She had set sail on little more than a dream. Like millions before her, she dreamed of a new life in a new place where all things might be possible. Her eyes blazed with longing of things to be: a loving husband, a home of her own, but most of all, Kinderleh, or children.

"How's my best girl?" I say in a hushed tone. It is Saturday and I whisper, "Good Shabbos, Grandma." She stirs and her head turns in my direction. She is calm, serene and at peace. There is no fear on her beautiful face.

"Good Shabbos, tatala," she answers in a barely audible voice. "You came here all the way from college? You didn't have to do that." She whispers, "Were you careful? You need to drive slowly. That little car is so small. I always worry."

She adored riding in my tiny MG with her babushka flying in the wind and the radio blaring. We would speed along the West Side Highway, bouncing over the cobblestones, passing great ocean liners berthed along the river. Those ships reminded her of a time long ago.

There is a lump in my throat. I want to speak, but I'm afraid if I do I will lose my composure. She squeezes my hand but there is very little strength left. A smile crosses her lips. Failing kidneys now spew poisonous toxins into her blood. There is no fear in her voice, no dread on her face. Even as she lay dying, Grandma is comforting me just as she has done all my life.

"Darling," she whispers, sensing my uneasiness. "No tears. I lived a long and wonderful life and I have seen so many wonderful things." Her fragile hand grasps tighter. "My children are all happy and healthy. My grandchildren will have long and healthy lives, and soon I will be again with Papa."

She stops to catch her breath. "You must always rejoice in life," she says. "Have no regrets. You will meet a girl someday. Your own Kinderleh will be like blazing candles in your life as you are to me. Go now, tatala. I don't want to see your tears. I love you." Her eyes close. She is asleep. I lean down and kiss her forehead. A faint odor of acetone escapes from her lips. The end is almost here. My lips linger a few seconds longer. I whisper softly into her ear and say goodbye to my beloved best girl.

At every turn, at each of life's crossroads, Grandma Tillie has been my anchor, the port that I could go to whenever life's storms tossed me about and threatened to capsize my boat. At first, I am frightened, scared of what it will be like without her. But then I remember what she has given me, given to all her children and to all her grandchildren: a roadmap—no—a treasure map to seek out our own happiness. Her steady hand and gentle voice have been her gift to me. I will be all right because she will be with me always.

I am on an elevator. A black man wearing a uniform with gold braid on the shoulders looks like something between a major general and a theater usher. He sits on a small stool attached to the wall. The brass accordion gate snaps shut. We descend and I am grateful to be the only passenger. I step out into the hospital's rotunda.

Dark rich wood paneling surrounds me. Framed portraits of hospital benefactors and doctors emeritus adorn the soaring walls. Splashes of light from high windows splay across an ornate terrazzo floor. I cross the expanse, hearing my heels click with each step. A doorman dressed like the elevator operator opens the wood portal for me and nods, beckoning me to pass through. Outside, a chill wind forces me to reach for my coat buttons and I remember when Grandma first taught me to button up. I walk down the four or five concrete steps as the cold, bright November sunlight sweeps across my face. At the bottom I turn and look up. In one of those rooms, my wonderful grandmother is slipping away from me, and from the life she loves so much. I know I will never see her again.

Strangely, sadness does not overcome me. I will not wail at her passing nor rend my garments, as is Jewish tradition. She would never want that. Instead, I will revel in her life, joyful for the years we shared. Someday I will tell my own children about the beautiful young girl who traveled across an ocean, found her beloved, and gave us all hope and a compass to find the way on our own turbulent seas.

Nothing Like a Good Laugh

The beginning of recovery can happen in an instant

Francine L. Baldwin-Billingslea

I T WAS A cold and blistery eve so Wilson and I decided to stay in and watch the big peach drop in Atlanta, Georgia. We counted with millions of people all over the world — 5-4-3-2-1 —and shouted out Happy New Year. We kissed, hugged and wished each other a safe, prosperous and healthy 12 months ahead. Later as I walked him to the door, he hugged me again and said, "I believe this is going to be a very special year." I smiled in agreement and told him to get home safely and I'd see him tomorrow.

I quickly ran upstairs to rub my aching left shoulder and arm with a muscle ointment. While rubbing, I promised myself that I'd make a doctor's appointment within the week to get a prescription for the nagging arthritis. I had already put it off too long. I didn't want to start the year full of aches and pains.

I kept my promise and got a thorough exam. I picked up my prescription and, other than the nagging arthritis, received a good report. My mammogram was scheduled for the following day and, once that was completed, I would be done with my yearly physical.

The next day, as I sat and waited for the slow moving technician, I tried to block out the nagging pain by thinking about shopping and painting the accent wall in the family room. As I stepped up to the machine, the technician positioned my right breast and tightened the plate. She ran behind a screen and shouted the orders, "TAKE A DEEP BREATH, HOLD AND RELAX." When she yanked and pulled my left side into position and started tightening the plate, sharp, intense pains danced up and down my arm, across my chest, shoulder, and upper back, and almost brought me down to my knees. After taking the picture and showing it to the doctor, I had to have the left side done over again. I was then escorted down the hall to have a sonogram, then down another hall to have a biopsy, and then sent home in pain to await the report, which came back three days later. I didn't have arthritis; I had a tumor that was stage two breast cancer. Less than two weeks later, I was recovering from surgery and waiting to start chemotherapy. Now the real battle was to begin.

The chemo was ruthless. I lost my appetite and weight, became nauseous, anemic, dehydrated and fatigued. I dealt with all of these, but when I began to lose my hair it was a brutal blow that sent me into a downward spiral of depression, hopelessness and a lack of desire to live. During this time, Wilson hardly left my side.

One day while I was attending the ultimate pity party, I looked in the mirror and a female version of Uncle Fester (from *The Addams Family*) stared back at me. I was bald, pale and bloated with deep dark circles around my eyes. Ashamed of the way I looked, I decided to tell Wilson that I was ugly and I looked like Uncle Fester. I didn't want him to see me looking this way and I didn't want to see him anymore. I told him to leave me alone and go find someone pretty and healthy with hair. To my surprise he said, "OK," and left. Thinking that I'd never see him again, I ran up to my room and cried myself to sleep. About an hour later, the sound of the doorbell woke me. I went to see who it was and there he stood, completely bald with an eyebrow missing. (I suspect he had second thoughts when it came to the brows.) He grabbed my hand, looked sternly into my eyes and said, "I don't care who you think you look like; you'll always be beautiful to me. And if you think you're ugly because you don't have any hair, then we're both ugly now and we both look like Uncle Fester, so we deserve each other."

I looked at him standing there, so serious and humble with his one eyebrow. He looked so silly all I could do was burst out laughing. We both laughed at our Uncle Fester looks until our stomachs hurt. That was the first time I had laughed like that in months. We laughed about it for weeks and still laugh about it to this day. Just the name I gave that look still makes me laugh. That laughter came from so deep within that I think it had some sort of healing powers. That whole situation was such a turning point for me.

Several weeks later, I passed out from dehydration, a spiking fever, dropping blood pressure and anemia. When I fell, my top teeth went through my bottom lip and jaggedly tore it apart, as if it were opened with a can opener. I was rushed to the hospital and the emergency room doctor used the wrong sutures. I was then rushed to my room where I was hooked up to several IVs and lay in and out of consciousness for several days, unaware of the fact that the sutures had dissolved in that time, leaving my lip lying open, three times its size and oozing pus. But what I can remember is, every time I opened my eyes, Wilson was standing over me saying, "Hey beautiful, your Uncle Fester misses you, wake up and talk to me."

Although I was too sick and weak to say anything, it always made me smile or chuckle before I drifted back to sleep. When I was able to get out of the bed, I went past the mirror to use the bathroom and I was absolutely horrified at myself.

Eight days later I was released from the hospital feeling much better, but looking the same. I wanted to stay behind closed doors and enjoy my pity parties. But Wilson always made me go out, taking me to dinner, the movies, the mall and all the places he knew I enjoyed going. Never once did he act ashamed of me. He walked beside me, ignoring the loud whispers and the bold-faced stares, holding my hand in his with his head held high as if he were with the most beautiful woman in the world. As much I wanted to hold my head down, I had to hold it up for him. We both looked a mess!

Wilson's love and support gave me a desire to live and the strength to fight. After awhile, how I looked on the outside no longer mattered to me. I wanted to be healed and to be just as beautiful on the inside as Wilson made me think I was on the outside.

My survival mode finally kicked in and I began to fight with everything I had; not only physically, but spiritually, mentally and emotionally until I won every battle and eventually the war. I drew enough strength from Wilson until I had enough of my own. Whereas my recovery was once slow, taxing and a real effort, my mending and healing started to become speedy and almost effortless. I wanted to live; I wanted to become a victor and not a victim, and whenever I was sent an invitation to a pity party, I turned it down. I no longer had time for them; they weren't a part of my survival kit.

My biggest setback had become my biggest setup for living, and I know humor and support also played imperative roles. They were the "thin threads," they made the difference.

In spite of all that I had gone through, it did turn out to be a special year because it was what I had gone through that made me a survivor.

Finding America in Atlanta

Irving Berlin will never be the same

John J. Lesjack

E YES FIXED STRAIGHT ahead, a troop of young men and women soldiers marched through Atlanta International Airport on their way to Fort Benning, Georgia. Carol Lee and I, two senior citizens, sat in comfortable chairs and watched. We had 20 minutes to wait before our flight left. The company guide crisply snapped out: "Just back from Iraq! Company A!"

People shouted and whistled their gratitude. Smiling travelers set down suitcases, purses and packages in order to vigorously applaud. American soldiers being shown appreciation and respect for serving their country brought water to our old eyes. We stood up and joined a crowd of travelers watching present-day soldiers in Army colors march over to waiting trucks. World War II journalist Ernie Pyle could easily have captured the contrasts in that scene.

A sudden calm followed their departure and seemed to signal a quiet life without troops until a second company, looking sharp, marched into the rotunda. Step, step, step echoed through the round stone building until we heard, "Company ... halt!" Soldiers stood ramrod straight until the

company commander said, "Fall out." A large crowd of waiting families scrambled over to find their loved ones.

Most of the soldiers had young women in pretty clothes
to hug and kiss. Some had no one. Often, parents brought
a young woman, plus two or three children, over for a final
expression of love before saying goodbye. Then we saw
Grandpa, Grandma, the little blond girl and the "Mommy
Soldier." The little girl wore a big green bow in her hair, a
fluffy white dress, little socks and black Mary Jane shoes. She
was about four years old.

When "Mommy Soldier" turned, smiled and opened her
arms, the little girl stopped, put her feet together and tried to
salute with her left hand. No one cared that she didn't touch
her eyebrow, or that it was the wrong hand. People watching
felt a rising compassion for that family and began to cry. Well,
we did, anyway. "Come here, Precious!" "Mommy Soldier"
called. The girl flew into Mommy's arms and Mommy kissed
and hugged her baby and said, "I'm gonna miss YOU!"
"Mommy Soldier" held onto her daughter tightly even as she
hugged her parents. Grandpa and Grandma got involved in
the goodbyes and promises to write, honoring their "Daughter
Soldier" as civilians have always honored outbound soldiers.
Carol Lee was crying with them. When word came that it was
almost time to "fall in," civilians backed off.

"Mommy Soldier's" tears flowed as she patted her daughter's blond hair one more time, wiped her baby's own tears,
gave her one last kiss and then, reluctantly, handed the girl to
Grandpa who presented the girl to Grandma. "Mommy
Soldier" stood erect, eyes forward. The guide barked,

"On their way to Iraq ... Company B!" On the command, "Forward ... march," "Mommy Soldier," looking sharp, left with her company. The little girl's salute was wasted. Only Carol Lee and I noticed it, but the crowd cheered, applauded and whistled at the departing soldiers.

Hustle and bustle, carts beeping, cash registers ringing, and other noises returned as the airport got back to business as usual. We held our positions, probably too emotionally drained to move, but we weren't the only ones with tears in our eyes. And then it happened! A heavyset man appeared in the center of the terminal floor, stood on the tiles and burst into *God Bless America* a cappella. While his high tenor voice rolled along the walls and travelers again got teary-eyed during "Land that I love/Stand beside her/ And guide her"— Hartsfield-Jackson International became as quiet as a library. Carts stopped beeping. Cash registers went silent. We had heard *God Bless America* hundreds of times before, but no one had made it sound more beautiful. "Through the night/ With the light/ From above!"

By the time he sang, "From the mountains," I didn't dare look at Carol Lee. I knew what she was feeling, that her whole face was wet, and she would soon have to sit down. I knew because I was pretty much the same way.

"To the prairies/ To the oceans/ White with foam," the man sang. Nearing the end of his performance, when he hit the high notes, the stranger might have been showing his musical range as he sang, "God bless America/ My home sweeeeet home." Then, in even higher notes, using the acoustics of the building and really showing off, he finished with "God bless

America/ My home sweeeeet home!" and a lot of people wept openly. I might have been one of them. Carol Lee might have been another.

And then the stranger left. Not only did people ask, "Who was that guy?" but they also asked, "Where did he go?" People wanted to thank him. (Questions later put to the airport office asking if they had hired a singer went unanswered.)

I doubt that anyone had heard a rendition of that Irving Berlin song so well done before. As the lyrics were dying out over the sobbing civilians, Carol Lee and I found our comfortable chairs and pulled ourselves together.

With the announcement of our flight, our visit was over. In the last few days, we had attended a wedding of some friends of Carol Lee's in south Georgia. We had visited with my old Navy buddy and his wife in Atlanta. We had stayed at a charming B & B where we had to pray with strangers before each meal but, more importantly, through our experiences, we had gotten in touch with America. We never looked at our country the same way again.

We drifted over to our departure gate, boarded the plane, and headed toward California and our safe "Home sweet home/ Close to an ocean with white foam..."

My Mother's Gift

Forever dancing in the light

Gary Luerding

THE DOCTOR WORE a somber expression on his face as he approached us in the waiting area of the emergency room. I gripped my wife Lynne's hand tightly and tried to stifle the tears that were welling in my eyes. He sat down beside us and said, "The x-rays show your mother's cancer has advanced rapidly. I told her we could operate or continue with the morphine and antibacterial drip. Her chances for survival are almost nil." I sputtered, "If the colon hadn't ruptured..." He just shook his head. "She wants to see you before she decides, but the decision has to be made quickly."

We followed the doctor into my mother's room. She looked up and smiled. She was always smiling, even in the face of adversity, but there had never been anything like this.

"I'll leave you alone," the doctor said and closed the curtain behind him.

"You heard?" she asked, as I sat down on the bed and took her hand.

I nodded. "I'm so sorry, Mom," I said my voice trembling.

"Guess he doesn't hold out much hope. He didn't come right out and say it, but I saw it in his eyes." Again, that weak smile.

29

Hope, I thought. Such a small word, but in this context it was a tenuous thread that, for the moment, was binding the three of us together in this sterile room.

This was the third year of the battle between my mother and colon cancer, and the cancer was winning. The only reason she wasn't in too much pain was because of the pain medication.

I took her hand in mine and she gripped it strongly.

"What should I do, Gary?"

How ironic that all my childhood Mom had made decisions for me. Even as an adult she would advise me to the extent that I resented it, but I knew she was only looking out for my best interest. Sometimes I heeded her advice; many times I did not. A few times I regretted it. Now the roles were reversed. Now, SHE was asking for MY advice, and I didn't have an answer.

"What should I do?"

"Mom, how can I make that decision for you? Please don't ask me to. This is something you must decide on your own."

She nodded. "But what would YOU do?" She wasn't going to let me out of it that easy. What could I tell her? Three years of fighting, several surgeries later, and it comes down to this.

From the time she was three years old and lost her left arm and leg in a trolley car accident, my mother had been a fighter. Things that we take for granted were extremely difficult for her, but she overcame those obstacles to become an accomplished musician, dancer and teacher.

She once told me that she didn't miss the loss of her limbs because it happened so many years ago. For her it was natural.

And she deplored the term, "physically challenged," preferring the use of "handicapped" instead.

In her youth, she had been the "toast" of San Francisco, playing the trumpet in an all girl symphony orchestra at the age of 16, and later headlining at the Curran Theater in a dance act with her sisters. Yet, she thought it was no big deal.

Mom couldn't believe people were amazed at her accomplishments and, for all her old publicity photos and news clippings, she told me the one she was most proud of was the one of the two of us in the hospital that appeared in the *San Francisco Examiner* several days after my birth.

All my life Mom had given me gifts, but it was the intangible ones that I learned to appreciate the most. By her own living example, she passed on to me her incurable optimism, perseverance, courage and fortitude. Yet, it took me a long time to realize these were the most important.

Now, 50 years later, we were once again in a hospital room together, only this time there were no photographers or reporters. No fame, no well wishes. It was just a mother who was dying and a son saying goodbye, and that terrible question, "What would YOU do?"

I wanted to scream out to her, "Mom, how can you lie in that bed, your insides riddled with cancer and STILL hold out hope when there IS none?" But that was the essence of my mother. Her entire life had been a challenge. This was just the latest of many, and she wouldn't give up without a darn good reason.

"What would you do, Gary?" she repeated.

"They are giving you a lot of stuff to fight the infection.

Why not give it a chance?" How could I tell her she was dying even though she knew?

She visibly relaxed at my words. "Yes. I think maybe you're right. Let's give it a chance."

Moments later, I was talking to the surgeon. "It's the right decision," he said. "If she had the operation, it would mean more suffering and the outcome would be the same. She wouldn't leave the hospital."

As the morphine took hold, she was without pain and wanted us to go home. She insisted she felt better and saw no point in our remaining with her. One thing I had learned a long time ago was that you didn't argue with my mother. Then she motioned for Lynne to sit on the bed. We both held her hand as she looked into our eyes.

"Love each other," she smiled, and then slowly closed her eyes in sleep.

We returned the next morning. "Mom?" No answer. The morphine held her in a deep sleep. Her breathing was labored with long pauses between breaths. After each exhale, I held my own breath, wondering if it would be her last.

The nurse asked if I wanted her revived so that I could talk with her. I said no. She was sleeping so peacefully that I couldn't allow her to awaken and realize her condition.

I couldn't stand seeing her like this, so I momentarily left the room and walked down the hall. Suddenly and unexpectedly, I felt her there — felt such an outpouring of love and peace that I was nearly overwhelmed by it. For a moment, I had to lean against the corridor wall for support before rushing back to her room to hear her raspy breathing.

"She's not here," Lynne said, her face streaked with tears, although under those tears was the look of peace. That feeling I had in the corridor had also been extended to my wife. It was then we both knew that, even though her body was alive, her spirit had departed. She was free. And, in my mind's eye I saw her as girl of 16, whole again, an expression of joy on her face as she danced, not for an audience, but joyously into the light of God's love. I believe this was her way of telling me that everything was all right.

It was her final gift.

The Alcoholic

People can change!

Milda Misevicius

WATCHED HIM. I always watched him.

As he stumbled; as he fell. As his nose bled and vomit dripped from his mouth. The front of his pants darkening with uncontrolled urination.

I watched out for him. Afraid at what I would see. Then I watched over him.

He was, after all, my father.

He repulsed me. Embarrassed me and humiliated me. Yet, I always did what I thought was my sole responsibility—I cleaned him up. Put him to bed. Hid the evidence from my mother. And kept vigil all night, praying and praying, for everything to be all right.

I do not remember knowing that there was a problem prior to that tender age of eight. Prior to that, I always felt secure. My world, as it related to me, was wonderful. I was happy.

But I do remember losing that feeling of peace, without actually knowing an exact moment or time. It was an instant that uncorked a perplexing emotional response—love and hate became a simultaneous daily event.

My heart was torn in two for a father who was loving, kind

and caring. How I loved that tender part of him. He was
funny and handsome. And I felt safe when he held me.

I hated the other side, when the demons came out. And
they came out quite often.

I was always diligent in keeping, or at least trying to keep, a
house that was in order, for the least little thing could unleash
the vile monster. I got great grades, was super tidy, super help-
ful. I never asked for anything. I never complained. At my
tender age, I was the anchor. As I saw it, I could fix this problem with my behavior, commitment and my communication
with God; a huge responsibility for a little girl.

Every Friday night, every holiday, any day was an excuse for
a drink. Every horrible birthday, every long weekend, every
sporting event was marred with fear and disappointment.
How I hated the justification for the drink.

The hugs and kisses would turn to scolding, pushing, verbal
abuse and, once in a while, the infliction of a physical lashing,
either by hand or belt.

And still, I could not hate him 100 percent.

And I could not love him 100 percent.

He would be guilty; he would be good. He would do a little
gesture that would up heave my heart and allow me to love
him. He would then take a drink, another one, and another
and the cycle of demon and devotion would continue.

How I would have preferred that he were a bastard! But he
too had a split soul. It was later in life that I realized that alcoholism is a disease and that there was nothing I could have
done to fix the situation or cure the illness.

I thought if I could do something drastic maybe my father

would see how this affected our family and stop drinking. He would realize how much pain his drinking caused and how hurtful his behavior was.

I had no other option. It was, of course, my role to perform the act that would allow this miracle.

The night was bitter. Torrential rain poured down, drenching everything in its path. Gutters overflowed, forming rivers on streets. Anything not secured was shoved aside by the mounting water. The wind howled relentlessly. Lightning crashed to the ground. The sound and fury of the tempest was at a boiling point, inside and out.

Tension was mounting in the house. My parents' voices were getting louder by the minute. His slurring became more prominent. Chairs were pushed aside—same story, different day. And I was going to put an end to it once and for all.

I ran into the kitchen. The table was overturned, dishes were flying, and food was clinging to the curtains. I looked at my parents and said, "I want to die." I meant the words, and stormed out into the storm.

Within seconds my little nightgown was soaked. I had on slippers that were washed off my feet by the force of the water forming mounds of puddles on the street. I ran into the night.

If I could die, they would have to make up at the funeral. "I hope I die ... I hope I die ... I hope I die." "I hope he dies ... I hope he dies ... I hope he dies." The words pounded in my head. A mantra of demise and dedication.

My soul was screaming. My heart throbbing. My eyes stinging from the piercing rain dissolving my tears synchronized with the downpour.

I ran to a park around the corner. Sat under the biggest tree—and pleaded to God to have the lightning strike me dead.

I shivered. I screamed in anguish. Yet God did not allow death to occur.

My mother found me; carried me home. Put me in the bath. Her eyes were nearly swollen shut from crying. She held me until the last of the fear exhausted its way out of my heart with unfathomed emotion.

I clearly saw the damage I had done to her. How scared she was. How much could she take? I was stupid, stupid, stupid. I was so sorry that my already broken heart shattered into a dozen broken pieces.

Turned out that my father didn't even know I was "missing." He fell down in the basement and did not move until the morning. I was not there taking care of him, as I had to take care of letting my mother take care of me.

She fell asleep holding me. And I vowed that I would always take care of both of them no matter what. I loved her. I loved my father.

I cursed God for not fixing the problem. Thanked Him for not letting me die. My mother needed me too. I was her comfort and joy.

Eventually a miracle did happen. My father stopped drinking. We did become a truly happy family. The last years of my parents' lives were filled with cuddles, laughter, peace, kind words and treasured memories.

During the time of my father's illness, prior to his death, he told me that he remembered my saying "I will always take care of you, Daddy."

And I did.

My mother and I never talked about the day of the storm; never had to. She knew what I was trying to do.

My father and I never talked about the days infused with alcohol and hatred. There was no reason to.

I had forgiven him.

And he had forgiven himself.

Stepping Stones to Heaven

How kindness changes lives

Joan Clayton

"THIS IS FOR you, Mrs. Clayton. I loved being in your second grade. I will miss you. I love you."

Bobby handed me a used Barbie doll that was wearing a make-do dress of red and yellow crepe paper. The doll stood in a glass vase to hold her intact. Red ribbons around the glass had two tiny hearts, tied together with chubby hands of love. One heart read, "Bobby"; the other, "Mrs. Clayton."

Did Bobby have to sacrifice something he loved to give me this gift? Did he trade something he treasured with his sister? Or maybe she just gave him the doll, even though the Barbie meant a lot to her. I just knew someone had to have made a great sacrifice.

"Un regalo con muchas gracias. Tu eres una maestra mas bueno." *A present with many thanks. You are the best teacher.* Bobby's parents handed me the card they had written in Spanish. Since they did not speak English, I marveled all the more at Bobby's achievements.

When they handed me a dollar bill, I almost lost control. With a heart of love, I received the gift of all gifts.

This proud papa and mama had supported me all year

with their presence at parent conferences, parties and other activities. We laughed a lot at my college Spanish tinged with a southern accent. Bobby's parents and I had become close friends. His score on the achievement test ranked highest in my class. Bobby excelled, not because his parents required it, but because he knew they loved him unconditionally.

The whole family, including Bobby's siblings, hugged me goodbye. The time I shared as part of Bobby's life had come and gone. I clung to this last class. I had decided to retire after 31 years in the classroom.

It has been 10 years since I turned in my keys to a room I thought belonged to me personally. My office at home is decked with memorabilia. Bobby's Barbie doll still stands atop my desk. My files contain love notes from those wonderful years with the children. Every May I relive the last days of school, wishing I could start all over again. I wonder how my former students are doing and how many are graduating.

The ringing telephone brought me back to reality.

"Hi, Mrs. Clayton. This is Bobby. Remember me? I was in your class the year you retired." Of course I remembered.

"Well, thank you Bobby. After 10 years you still remember me?" I asked, amazed.

"I could never forget you, Mrs. Clayton," he said "I'm calling to see if you could come to my high school graduation. It's Saturday afternoon at one o'clock."

"Thank you so much for asking. Of course my husband and I will be there," I answered. I pictured my little Bobby, grown up and graduating from high school. And he still remembered me.

Emmitt and I left early since the high school was a distance away in another town. I told him all the wonderful things I remembered about Bobby and his family. He could hardly wait to meet them.

Once there, we found a seat and began to read our program. "Look!" I exclaimed. "Bobby is valedictorian." I was so proud of him. But, of course, I always knew he had great potential.

Bobby gave a marvelous valedictorian address. He told of the wonderful heights to be achieved, the persistence for seeking the good, doing the right thing and never giving up. I beamed with pride.

Bobby then retold his speech in Spanish since several non-English-speaking parents were in attendance.

When he had finished, I heard Bobby say, "Now I want to honor a person who has had a profound effect upon my life. She set me on a path in second grade that has enabled me to succeed."

He reached under the podium and pulled out a big cuddly teddy bear. "Mrs. Clayton, this is for you." He walked off the stage and came toward me. I ran to meet him, crying all the way. We hugged for a long time while the audience clapped.

After the ceremony, Bobby's dad walked up to me with a bouquet of yellow carnations and a card written in Spanish. In the midst of all the hugging, I kept hearing him say, "Gracias maestra." While I didn't always keep up with my Spanish, his language and his eyes spoke volumes of love.

At home that night, I opened the beautiful card. I read it slowly in Spanish, savoring every word.

"In the fight of life there is much pain and tears, but

someone comes into your life whose love heals the hurt." It was signed by Bobby's dad.

"You taught him to read. You taught him to sing. Here is a kiss from all of us for teaching our precious son." This sentiment was signed by Bobby's mom.

I was the happiest ex-teacher in the world. Bobby and his parents not only taught me the value of friendship, but also demonstrated love in action.

Bobby and his parents became my teachers. They taught me a wonderful concept: friendship and love are stepping stones on the way to heaven.

The Tooth Fairy

Sometimes we have to believe in the impossible

Dean F.H. Macy

I N DECEMBER OF 1945 I celebrated my ninth birthday. It was a small party. Mary Lou and Howie came and, of course, the adults: my mother, my Aunt Emma and Uncle Charlie. Aunt Emma baked me a cake with real butter frosting. I felt special. Butter was rationed and expensive, which meant she had to have put a little away each week just for me.

My presents were mostly homemade. Aunt Emma gave me a long knitted scarf and matching sweater. Uncle Charlie had whittled out a whistle with three holes so I could change the pitch. And my mother gave me (wonder of wonders) a chemistry set.

Ever since I saw one in Gilbert's window two years before, I had wanted a chemistry set. That was on my seventh birthday. My mother had taken me to Gilbert's so I could pick out a Lionel train set. It was another one of those special birthdays from Mom that I never forgot. She used most of her month's government check on that train set. But that was then.

One day in early spring after my seventh birthday I came home from school and discovered my mother sitting on the sofa crying. My mother never cried in front of me. Well, she

43

did when she saw a sad movie or read something "tender" in a book, but I never saw her really cry. I was scared. She put her arm out and drew me close and through her sobs she kept repeating, "Oh, honey. Oh, honey," over and over. In her hand she held a yellow paper with writing on it. I never forgot the few words I saw, "United States" and "Army" and "sorry" but nothing else. That autumn, the checks stopped forever.

Mom began to clean houses and she made fancy cookies and sold them during the holidays at Rockefeller Center. I became a choir boy at St. James Church and got paid $21 a week to sing.

And then, two years later, even with our trying to scrape out a living, I got the chemistry set I'd always wanted. She smiled at me and I saw my aunt and uncle's smiling faces. I said, "But ... how?"

"It wasn't us," Aunt Emma protested. "Your mother did this all by herself." She patted my head. I was too excited to let that pat bother me. Again I looked at my mother. "But, Mother, it's impos—"

And then mother told me something she had often said in the past but that didn't hit home until then. "Honey, remember when your father ... left ... I told you that we'd be all right?" I remembered. She said that nothing was impossible to those who believed, that if they believed something good would happen it became possible. I don't think I did much believing but obviously she did.

I opened my new chemistry set under the watchful eyes of my mother. There were boxes of chemicals and two boxes of litmus paper, red and blue, and five test tubes in a wooden test tube holder, tweezers, a test tube brush, a metal spoon and eye dropper, some cleaning tissues and five corks. I carefully removed and examined each new offering. Under the boxes of chemicals were pamphlets, which my mother said she'd help me to understand, and a chart showing how to do experiments.

One of the diagrams showed a test tube being held over the flame of an alcohol lamp. I looked for the lamp. I found the wire stand but there was no alcohol lamp. I realized my mother was watching me.

"I ... I couldn't get one this time," she said, "but perhaps ... when things get better, maybe we can ..." She trailed off. For a moment I felt cheated. Then I thought about that impossible stuff and told her that it was OK, that I could use a candle to heat the test tubes. She looked relieved and happy again.

My one and only ever chemistry set lasted 11 years. I was very careful to use only what was needed for an experiment; never more. After I finished playing with it, I'd let the alcohol lamp cool off before I capped it and put it and everything else back in the hinged, metal box where it belonged, snapping the two pieces shut.

Yes! I got the alcohol lamp. It was several months after my memorable birthday. I went ice skating with Howie Schwartz. My skates hit a twig and stopped moving. I landed face down on the hard ice and broke a tooth where it went into the gum. I cried. Howie helped me get home and my mother took me to a dentist in our building. He said he'd have to remove the tooth.

I never had a dentist remove a tooth before. That was when

I learned to hate dentists. I was scared. I cried a lot. I bit the dentist's thumb. But eventually the tooth was out. He rinsed it and held it up for me to take. He said that the tooth fairy ought to give me a generous offering for a tooth that big.

"All I want is an alcohol lamp," I thought to myself. I had never again asked for it. I realized that money was tight and I'd probably never own one. Besides, candles did work OK although they smudged the glass.

So that night, although I knew better, I put the remains of the tooth under my pillow. "Believe the impossible," my mother had said. So I did, although I had already discovered who the elusive tooth fairy was on the last tooth. So now I knew and my mother knew that I knew. But I really wanted the alcohol lamp. So, I told the make-believe tooth fairy what I wanted and went to sleep.

The next morning I reached under my pillow. The tooth was gone. There was no reward there either. I searched in the pillow case for my tooth or the money but found nothing. "Great," I thought. "Someone snatched my tooth!" I decided to get up and ask my mother why she'd taken the tooth. I leaned over the side and peered under the bed as I did every morning to make sure there were no monsters there. No monsters were—but something else was under the bed, lying in the dust.

It was a small brown box. There were no markings on it. A strange feeling came over me as I wrapped my fingers around it. When I lifted it up I could not see any dust where it had lain. It was as if the box had been there all the time and the dust had slowly built up around it. Well I knew it wasn't there yesterday. I had looked. I brought it up and put it on my bed and stared at it. I was almost afraid of what might be in it.

As I sat there staring, mother came in and asked me what the box was. I told her that she should know; she put it there. But somehow I knew that she hadn't. Of course she said she'd never seen the box before. I believed her. My mother had never lied to me. I opened the box and pulled out a very old alcohol lamp. The glass was hand blown and thick. The wick assembly looked like brass and the cap was the same but tarnished. It was beautiful. Mother and I polished it until it gleamed like gold.

Where did it come from? I never knew. But to this day I believe that it was a gift from the real tooth fairy, the one who comes when someone is ready to believe in the impossible.

The Bundled Gift

Choosing each other

Kathe Campbell

NINE MONTHS HAD run into 10 during the medically unsophisticated days of our country's Great Depression in the early 1930s. Yet with each weekly checkup my parents listened impatiently to the doctor's unconcerned response: "Don't worry about it, folks, I've had several new mothers fill out a 10-month term."

My father delighted in their home, his tailor-made suits, and a new car every fall. His glorious tenor was his trademark as he conducted Easter sunrises and poured his heart into community service. His proud name still encircles the archway of the boys' orphanage he founded after the devastating stock market crash. But best of all, an abiding love for God and family reigned as he shed his striped serges and grey flannels on weekends and was completely at home washing the cars or manicuring the yard.

Mom was no bigger than a minute, a born cook, gardener and hostess. Men gushed with envious stares as dad whirled his dark-haired Irish beauty around the floor at their monthly dance club. She played piano and organ at church, enjoyed bridge with the girls, and sang contralto at St.Cecilia's. They were big-city dwellers with a fenced-in backyard, an enormous willow tree, a fish pond, a dog and a cat—but no child.

My folks were ecstatic over thoughts of their first baby but after eight years had nearly given up. Now the surgically frocked doctor soberly rendered my poor dad an unthinkable choice in the father's waiting room. "Either the child or your wife; I'm so sorry," he solemnly announced.

As Caesarian sections were a rarity back then, their lovely dark-haired daughter died at birth and my parents were left to grieve. Mother would face many weeks recovering from the almost impossible delivery. Furthermore, she bitterly faced the thought of never again bearing a child to take home to the yellow nursery the couple had so lovingly created.

Dad handled the simple funeral arrangements alone and in agony. The baby was laid to rest next to her maternal grandmother with a simple prayer and a flood of tears coursing down his cheeks. It was crushing as he told his beloved of the woeful day, clutching flowers in trembling hands while they held each other tight in the bleak, white hospital room.

Each week slid by routinely for my father. He went to work and visited with Mom, cheering her days with bouquets of violets and wisps of the baby's breath she so adored. He then went home and would ascend the stairway to where the bright and lonely nursery still awaited its child. In misery, he lay in bed at night unable to sleep while hopes of fulfilling the couple's destiny seemed lost forever. Thoughts of adopting a child began invading his dreams and awakenings. But was he too old at 44?

He soon began spending evenings at the Children's Home,

where it was rumored they had to sweep him off their porch each morning. Although most Depression families were saddled with overwhelming hardships, Dad had job security, babies were plentiful, and he started adoption proceedings immediately.

My father would have to be blind not to notice the smiling wide-eyed girl baby with just a hint of red hair so different from his own lost infant. The ladies crowed loudly to him upon his visits. "She's a very healthy, happy three-month-old, Sir, and she has a wonderful disposition—our best recommendation amongst so many."

He visited all the babies often, but always returned to my shameless and playful flirtations, craving his unconditional love. He had become smitten, even before discussing the idea with Mom. They would have their child to take home.

Christmas Eve only a day away, and mother looking and feeling considerably more fit, Dad once again sought out her doctors. "She needs to be home and we see no reason why she shouldn't care for a baby—with much help, of course," they agreed.

The plan in motion, Dad raced to the Children's Home to make arrangements for a judge to preside over the paperwork and for a temporary live-in nurse. No man could have been more exuberant or passionate at the thought of introducing me to the woman who was to be my mother that very evening.

They sipped wine, held hands, and talked excitedly across a candlelit table in the most fashionable spot in town that Christmas Eve of 1932. After dinner, Dad nervously escorted his beloved up the steps of the gray-stoned building and, at the appointed hour, entered the hushed and dismally out-dated reception room. Almost immediately a nurse appeared and placed me in the arms of my father. Without hesitation, I smiled up at his familiar face, cooing and flailing my arms and legs in utter joy. My parents' jubilant and tear-filled eyes met for the supreme moment when Dad placed his gift into my mother's outstretched arms.

Pure exultation pervading her very being and a thousand butterflies fluttering aimlessly up her spine, she looked long-ingly at my father and whispered, "Oh, honey, she's so tiny and beautiful—is she really ours?"

Now 76 years have left me with this beautiful story told a thousand times—precious memories of adoring parents who wanted me more than anything. My father had taken the bull by the horns to soothe a tattered soul and awaken his tena-cious spirit. It matters not our days and years together, our typical highs and a few lows, for being his daughter was ulti-mate bliss. He had chosen me and I chose him.

Wave of Solace

Message from the sea
Caesaria, Israel - February 2000

June Can

I WAS WALKING ALONE along the beach, contemplating and taking pictures. I had come to say goodbye to one of my favorite places in Israel, the beach of the Roman Aqueducts in Caesaria. It was a cold winter morning. I had driven out there by myself to spend some time with the sea.

I had a lot on my mind and in my heart. My family was moving to America. My husband was already there, and my two children and I were going to him on February 16.

I had agreed to leave Israel, where I had lived for 32 years, to try and have a better life in America. My husband was very much for it. My children were not that enthusiastic, but had somewhat gotten used to the idea.

I had moved to Israel from America at the age of 11. I knew what acclimatizing to a new country and culture meant. As the mother in the family, I knew we were in for a real ride of both adventure and hardship. I was scared of what lay ahead.

The Mediterranean Sea had always been my solace and connection point with my higher power. That huge body of water with its constant rolling waves was like an ever-present portrayal of Mother Earth. Writing the words "Mother Earth" in the sand, I counted seven waves before the words were washed away by the foaming salty water.

I knew I was leaving my biological mother and three sisters in Israel. They would not be in America with me. I leaned against the aqueduct and tears started to roll down my face. I loved my family and the land of Israel, and leaving them both was hard for me. I felt as if I were being torn away like Velcro.

"Help me Mother Earth," I prayed. "Help me through this mighty transition. I am leaving my family, and Israel," I sobbed.

It started to drizzle and I wrapped my winter coat around me and put up my hood. I lifted up my head and looked at the sea. The huge body of water looked alive, tossing and turning amidst the rain and the waves.

"I stretch from the shores of Israel to the shores of America," I heard it say. "I am your constant connection between America and Israel. If you put your finger in the water you can feel the coast on the other side."

I rushed to the frothing water and stuck my finger in and imagined my energy going to the coast of America. I felt the connection. I realized then that when I was in America, living in Connecticut, all I would have to do is put my finger in Long Island Sound and feel the connection to Israel and my family.

This realization somehow made the move less traumatic for me. I knew that I was not falling off the planet. Up until that moment I felt as if I were being uprooted and going to a totally different world. Somehow this realization of the water connection between the continents of Asia and North America made them seem less far apart to me.

I also realized that Mother Earth, whom I always saw through water, would be with me in America. There too I could go to her and rest in her arms. Even though I was leaving my biological mother, my Earth Mother would be with me in America.

I dried my tears. The rain stopped and the sun came out. I stood saying my last goodbye to the beloved sand and water and again felt my higher power speaking to me.

"Stay positive and good things will come to you," it said.

I struggled against my fear and dread for a moment. Then, feeling strong from my connection with Mother Earth, and knowing she would be a constant presence in my life no matter where I lived on the planet, I made a decision. I decided to stay positive and keep a grateful attitude throughout our move.

This morning at the sea gave me strength and courage to face uprooting myself and my family from the land of Israel. It gave me the conviction to face the challenges in our new life in America with a positive outlook and to appreciate everything as much as I could.

In retrospect I see that my internal transition from a negative thinker to a positive thinker started that day on the beach. There I made my first steps toward learning to steer my thoughts in a positive direction. This internal shift not only helped me in the move to America, it helped me change my whole outlook on life.

Forever Sharp

The teacher who rescued Terri Termite

Terri Elders

"No one can make you feel inferior without your consent."
ELEANOR ROOSEVELT

"**P**SSST! HEY, TERMITE! Pssst!"

Glen and Jimmy were at it again, hissing like a pair of rabid rattlesnakes. I wished I could stick my fingers in my ears to tune them out. But maybe they were right, I thought. I actually did chew my pencils to pieces. I guessed I really was just a termite, just an insect.

"You've got to ignore them," my big sister, Patti, had advised. "Don't pay them any attention whatsoever."

I tried to follow her advice. Though in 1945 we were only eight and nine, Patti already knew how to handle boys. Nobody ever called her anything worse than Pinup Patti or Cover Girl, which she'd reward with a wink, a saucy remark, or a flirtatious toss of her curls.

I didn't want their attention at all. Boys just made me blush and hang my head. When they'd start to taunt, I'd fight the urge to sniffle or to stick my thumb in my mouth. I was convinced that boys were a separate species, like ring-tailed monkeys or Martians. They certainly couldn't be human.

"Terry Termite, Terry Termite," Glen and Jimmy continued to chant. I opened the lid of my school desk and peered inside. I wished I could shrink myself enough to jump right inside and pull the lid down over me. Instead I tossed in the gnawed remains of my old pencil, took out a fresh one, and then slammed down the lid with enough force that Miss Magee turned from the blackboard, where she had been posting our homework assignment.

"What's going on?" Miss Magee looked directly at the boys in the back of the room. I swung my head around just in time to catch Glen's gap-toothed grin as he widened his eyes, a sure sign he was about to tell a whopper.

"Nothing. Terry asked if she could see our multiplication tables. She still doesn't get the sevens and eights."

Sure, I struggled with multiplication, but even Miss Magee would know how improbable it would be for me or anyone else to ask either Glen or Jimmy for assistance with schoolwork of any kind. When I helped Miss Magee pass out corrected papers, I'd noticed the red marks that crisscrossed their pages. I might ask them how to harness a mule or skin a rabbit, maybe, if my life depended on it, but arithmetic? No way.

"I thought I heard hissing." Miss Magee took off her glasses and shook her head. "That doesn't sound like nothing to me. And somehow I doubt that Terry asked to see your work."

I just froze with embarrassment. I didn't want the whole room to hear this. That would just mean more boys teasing me later. I caught myself just in time as I moved my pencil towards my mouth. If only I could stop chewing them, I thought, maybe the boys would stop calling me Terry Termite. I smiled weakly, and then started to use the pencil to copy down our homework assignment.

After the bell rang, Miss Magee stopped me as I neared the door.

"I received two apples today. Let's sit outside for a while and eat them."

I nodded. Often Miss Magee would invite one or the other of us to share a few minutes after school. I was always happy to be singled out. We walked over to the playground and sat at the picnic table. I took a few deep breaths of the crisp late autumn air and wondered what we'd talk about this time. Once it had been about my penmanship, which, like my multiplication, was not too good. Another time it had been about my book report on *Dandelion Cottage*, which was really good.

As we munched, Miss Magee reached into her pocket.

"Once you get into sixth grade and move on to Room Three, you'll be using ink pens," she began. "But for now, I want you to have this."

She showed me a slim round silver piece of metal. I didn't know at first what it was.

"It's an Eversharp, a mechanical pencil," she said. "I'll show you how it works." She clicked a tiny button at one end, and a little piece of lead emerged from the other end. "The point never gets blunt, so it never needs sharpening. And when you run out of lead, there are more pieces stored in the case."

She handed me the pencil. I caressed the silver tube. It wouldn't be anything I'd want to put in my mouth and chomp. I was content just to stroke it.

"I think you're going to be a writer when you grow up," Miss Magee continued. "I'm never going to be able to give you an A in penmanship, since you write all over the paper instead of on the lines. But what you write is fresh and thoughtful. I'd like to see you write about pencils for your next essay. I'll enjoy watching the boys while you read it out loud."

I stared at the instrument. Could it be true? Could I break my gnawing habit?

Right away the new Eversharp began to work its magic. Whenever I felt nervous, I'd just caress it with my thumb. Within a day or two the hisses behind me had ceased.

A week later I stood before the class, paper in hand.

"My essay is called *Pencils and Pencil Heads*," I announced. Nobody laughed, but I thought I saw Glen and Jimmy begin to squirm.

Now, 60 years later, I don't recall the exact words of my effort, but I acknowledged having a bad habit of chewing on my pencils when I was nervous. I remembered stressing how lucky we were that pencils have erasers so that we can undo our mistakes. I contrasted that with real life, where our mistakes have a more permanent impact and can do serious harm. I alluded to name-calling as an illustration, and I'd glanced meaningfully towards the rear of the room.

Thanks to Miss Magee, I think I had made my point. Jimmy and Glen gave me no more than a quick nod when I returned to my desk. No hisses, no evil grins. The days of Terry Termite were over.

Soon, though, I heard taunts related to a popular comic

strip of the day, *Terry and the Pirates*. I wanted to be a pirate even less than I'd wanted to be a termite. Miss Magee helpfully suggested I change the spelling of my nickname to Terri, to make a better pair with my sister's name, Patti.

Ever sharp, that Miss Magee! She changed my life forever.

A Father's Words

It's never too late to experience love

Tracy Austin

THE BAD NEWS came along with the cold wind of a late season Nor'easter. My sister, Diane, was on the phone, telling me that our father had cancer again—melanoma. Even the name sounded evil. It was the same cancer he had three years ago and had undergone minor day surgery to remove. He had had other skin cancers as a young man, which he acquired while installing telephone cable in the hot South Texas sun. But none were potentially fatal until now.

"The doctors said that the skin cancer has metastasized. It's in four organs and it's inoperable." Diane was good at giving bad news. She had grace under pressure.

"I thought they got it all last time. Are they sure?" I was in shock. It was too big for me to wrap my mind around. Being the baby of the family, I had a childlike belief that our family would always be healthy and live forever.

"Yes, they are sure. The x-rays show tumors on his lungs, liver, lymph nodes and spleen. They said there is an experimental treatment, but he may not qualify because he is 65." Diane tried to sound hopeful.

"What difference does that make? Is his life worth less

because he is 65?" My voice cracked as the news began to sink in. My dad was going to die. It wasn't an "if"; it was a "when."

"No, it isn't, sweetie. This has been hard on us all. Dad is taking it well, though. He said he is going to fight this thing any way he can. He's going to a specialist on Monday."

"How's Mom doing?" My heart felt heavy with the thought of her losing the love of her life. They met, fell in love and married more than 42 years earlier. Their love was a rock; the very foundation of our family.

"She's all right, I guess. She always seems strong," Diane answered.

"I'm coming home," I said. "I'll find out when I can get a flight and I'll let you know." I had no idea how I was going to manage to keep this promise. I was living in Boston and barely able to make ends meet. I certainly didn't have the $1,200 for a round-trip ticket on short notice. The full fare would have been more than $2,000, but I was quoted the "family emergency" airfare after pleading my case to the reservations agent.

As I lay in bed that night, I listened to the wind howl outside. It was as if nature was crying with me. Somehow, I fell into a dreamless sleep despite my anxiety.

When I woke up the next morning, I knew that somehow life would provide a way for me to see my father. And when my new friend, Laurie, called later that day, my belief was confirmed. As she listened to me talk about my father and my struggle to find a way home, she offered her help.

"I can get you there," Laurie asserted with confidence.

"You can?" My words choked me. I was fighting back tears during the entire conversation and the dam was about to break.

"Yes, even though I'm retired I still get friends and family fares at American Airlines. You'll have to fly standby, but you can have my discount if you want it."

Laurie made all of the arrangements and even took me to the airport the next morning. The ticket cost only $115, which I could afford. As the plane left Boston, I watched the sun rise over the harbor. My hope rose with it.

A few hours later, we landed in St. Louis where I would change planes for Austin. I had forgotten that the South by Southwest Music Festival was starting that day and every musician in the lower 48 was trying to get there, too. Every flight was filled to capacity, and, since I was flying on a pass, I was not a priority for the airline.

As the day wore on and more flights came and left, I began to realize that getting home that day might not happen. I had lived in Boston for a few years, but I still had a small-town mindset, and sleeping alone in a major airport was a frightening prospect.

"Dad, it's me." I called from a pay phone in the airport. "I'm stuck in St. Louis and they don't know when I will be able to get a flight there."

"Well, what are you going to do?" Hearing his voice helped me to relax.

"I don't know. I've been running from gate to gate, trying to get on any flight going that way. But so far I've had no luck. I may have to spend the night here."

"Hmmmm." He took a deep breath and then sighed. "You know, I never worry about you."

"Really? Why not?" I was genuinely surprised to hear this.

"Because I know that whatever happens, you are a smart, capable woman and you'll be fine. No matter what roadblock you hit, you always find a way."

My heart warmed as I absorbed the sentiment of his words. "OK, Dad; I love you. I'll call you when I get there."

His words found a home deep within me. I guess I always knew he believed in me. He raised me to be who I am. What I didn't know was how profoundly his confidence in me would shore up my belief in myself. I consider that conversation one of the greatest gifts I have ever received.

I did find a flight late that night. It was the last seat on the last flight to San Antonio and that was close enough for me. Diane picked me up and drove me to Austin. My whole family was gathered together the next morning when Dad and I went for a walk. I don't remember everything we talked about. I do remember being with him and the comfort I found just talking to him about nothing at all.

That was more than 12 years ago. Since then, I have overcome many challenges. Whether it is a health, financial or spiritual trial, I hear my father's words of assurance again. They rise up from that place inside me where he planted them that night at the St. Louis airport, they bloom into the strength I need to keep tackling those roadblocks, and they continue to rise above the troubles of the day. He reminds me that I can achieve whatever I set out to do. And, he reminds me that I am loved.

That '50s Kind of Love

Memories of a drive-in movie

Lee Williams

YOU CAN LOOK, but you won't find them anymore. Throughout the country, they are buried underneath shopping malls, parking lots and apartment buildings, and yet they still flicker in my mind. The screens glowed from afar on lone highways; gigantic beautiful people moved in the dark, speaking words that were inaudible, unless you pulled in close and balanced a clunky speaker on the edge of your car window. This is what my family did on those sticky hot summer nights of my youth.

I remember one of those nights in particular. I remember it because the drama between my father and mother was much more exciting than that on the big screen swallowing up the darkness in front of me. The year was 1957. A lion roared, credits rolled, music filled up all the spaces between rows and rows of cars and then it all began—the story. On this night it was "The King and I." My sister and I huddled on a blanket next to the car under the stars. My eyes moved with the actors, frame by frame, mesmerized by it all, until my sister poked me in the side. "Hey, look at Mom and Dad."

We both stared, frozen on our homemade quilt. We didn't

move because we didn't want the moment to disappear. My father had his arm wrapped around my mother, who was snuggled in close. He leaned over and kissed her quickly, and she nuzzled even closer. It was rare for me to see such affection between them. They were usually shy and reserved with one another—two people who had come through the Depression and a war, two people who had started a life together with nothing more than a record player, a sofa and a bed. Like the drive-in theaters that slowly slipped away, their generation is vanishing and soon will be gone.

My father glanced down at us staring up at him. "You girls watch the movie," he said with a smile.

We immediately turned our heads and stared at the screen. But something inside of me was dancing—dancing like Deborah Kerr and Yul Brynner danced on the big wide screen that night. I lay there caught up in my parents' love for one another, and as their child, it made me feel grand and somehow safe. I cherished that drama, the validation that I came to be because at one time two people loved each other.

This truth was defined for me on that summer night, something I unconsciously recorded as I looked up at my parents and saw their silhouettes entwined in the sputtering light of a drive-in theater. And even when the movie was over and we sleepily collapsed in the back seat and Daddy turned in the speaker at the drive-through office and we raced down Highway 45 toward home, my mother was still cuddled up beside my father. The windows were rolled down, the wind was whipping my hair all around and the radio was playing Fats Domino. There had never been a moment of such security.

Sometimes later, when days were hard at my house, my father and mother were fighting too furiously, the dog was barking too loudly and my sister was pinching me too hard, I would purposely think about that night at the drive-in theater. It was a time that represented love, a time that represented the hope that even if things were bad, life could be that way again. Perhaps. It is something I needed to believe then and still need to believe now. It is that kind of love that can take your breath away—that shy, innocent, almost-cheesy, feel-good kind of love, that widescreen kind of love, a '50s kind of love.

Many things have been lost since that night at the drive-in. My parents are now buried in a cemetery close to the house where I grew up. I keep their pictures scattered throughout rooms in my home—pictures of their younger selves. They are memorials to that hope and commitment. The drive-in theater in that southern town has been demolished, and in its place, overgrown weeds sway like lovers underneath a blanket of stars. But sometimes today, when the kids are arguing too loudly, or my husband is working too busily, or the stuff of life weighs too heavily, I close my eyes and remember the gift of hope my parents gave me that night, and the song by Rogers and Hammerstein from that long-ago movie still echoes in my mind:

"Hello young lovers, whoever you are, I hope your troubles are few. All my good wishes go with you tonight, I've been in love like you."

The Papal Tablecloth
The most special occasion

Annmarie B. Tait

W ITH MANY EMPTY hours to fill after my boyfriend
enlisted in the Navy, I often spent my weekends
shopping at yard sales. I shopped more for the company
than the merchandise, but still the occasional fantastic "find"
always left me feeling victorious.

Such was the case one day when I found, strewn among
a pile of stained and shopworn linens, a pristine white satin
damask tablecloth with 12 matching napkins. Upon closer
inspection, I realized that these fine linens had never once
been released from the pink satin ribbon that wound around
them and rested on top in a never untied, ever so delicate,
miniature bow. The sight of it took my breath away. Tucked
inside, face down, under the ribbon was the price tag and my
hand trembled as I reached for it. Slowly I turned it over to
reveal $10 in black magic marker under which was written
"FIRM PRICE."

Ten dollars was quite a sum for a yard sale item 30 years
ago and I admit I had to empty my change purse and all of
my pockets to come up with the full amount. But any fool
could see this was a bargain beyond compare. With giddy

anticipation I watched as the woman counted my coins and then placed the tablecloth and napkins into a tattered shopping bag and handed it over to me.

As I meandered home I don't think my feet ever touched the ground. Floating high above the clouds, I daydreamed about all the lovely Thanksgiving dinners that would be celebrated around that tablecloth with crisply folded napkins anxiously waiting to dab happy mouths once I was married and in a home of my own.

How I loved tending to holiday dinners with my mother as I was growing up! She taught me well all the secrets of mouth-watering candied sweet potatoes (it's a teaspoon of cider vinegar amid all that butter and brown sugar that makes the difference) and light, fluffy melt-in-your-mouth biscuits. As much as I loved eating Thanksgiving dinner, the better pleasure for me was helping my mother and observing the care she took with everything she did in the kitchen.

Mom never learned how to sew, knit or crochet. In fact, crafts of any kind held no interest for her. She didn't belong to any clubs, play sports, nor was she active in the PTA. Mom poured every ounce of energy she had into caring for her family of seven, starting with every meal that went on the table.

Every step of the way back to my apartment I pictured all of our holiday treats shimmering like jewels on a canvas of snow-white satin damask. I could almost smell the turkey roasting! The harrowing thought of a cranberry stain snapped me back to reality just as I reached my apartment door and I flew up the steps, two at a time, energized by my good fortune and the satisfaction of one "fantastic find."

The very next weekend I went over to my mom's to show her my treasure. She too was quite taken by the pristine condition and wasted no time gushing over the beauty of it. As much as my mother loved to set a pretty table, I never remember her enjoying the pleasure of brand-new table linens. Though always clean and pressed, the telltale faded stains often exposed their hand-me-down rummage sale status. In a family of seven, extra cash wasn't easy to come by and would never have been spent on anything as frivolous as a new tablecloth.

The calendar pages flipped and in a few years I was married and living 3,000 miles from home. My husband and I shared our first Thanksgiving dinner with 10 sailors, all of whom were far from their own families. I called home to Mom several times that day with one supposed turkey crisis after another but I'm pretty sure she saw right through me. How I missed seeing her in her organdy apron she only wore on special occasions! When it was time to set the table for dinner, I didn't have the heart to use my lovely linens without my mother being there to appreciate them.

In fact, year after year, even after we came home to Philadelphia I still saved the linens for just the right "special occasion," having purchased and discarded several new cloths of lesser quality in the meantime. Somewhere along the line my husband launched a volley of jokes about how my grand tablecloth would never come out of storage until the Pope himself graced us with his presence for dinner. From that moment on it was known as the "Papal Tablecloth."

It wasn't long after the "Papal Tablecloth" earned its nickname that my sweet mother was diagnosed with lung cancer for the second time. At this point it was inoperable. She had already lost a lung to cancer seven years prior to this most recent diagnosis. The news arrived just before Halloween. It just so happened that it was my turn to host the rapidly approaching Thanksgiving.

The weeks between Halloween and Thanksgiving were inundated with consultations, additional biopsies, lab tests and one medical intrusion after another, all in an attempt to lengthen my mother's life. All along the way I hoped beyond hope for a miracle, and never fully came to terms with the finality of the inevitable.

Overwhelmed with fear and sorrow, I faced the task of cooking Thanksgiving dinner, wondering how I would ever get through it. Looking back I realize that it was clearly God's plan to keep me in the dark about the full extent of her condition. I invested all of my hope in the talk of "new medications" and "state of the art" treatments and drew from that my strength to keep the occasion light and happy. I believed with all my heart that this would not be her last Thanksgiving.

As you might have already guessed, the "Papal Tablecloth" was removed from its wrappings and graced our dining room table looking absolutely stunning dressed with the fine china handed down to me from my grandmother.

When Mom saw it on the table she once again gushed with praise just as she did so many years ago when I made a special trip home just to show it to her. As she traced the outline of the damask leaves with her finger she looked up at me with a broad but frail smile and said, "Don't tell me the Pope is finally coming for dinner!" To the sound of resounding laughter we all sat down and enjoyed turkey with all the trimmings. My mother raved about every dish but I noticed she hardly ate a morsel.

Exactly 99 days from the date she was diagnosed, Mom passed away. The debut of the "Papal Tablecloth" took place on what turned out to be her last Thanksgiving, as hard as my heart tried to deny it.

If the Pope ever does come for dinner at our house, I'll use the fine linen. I really don't think he'll mind a faded stain or two.

Paid Not To Golf

Good china isn't just for the holidays

Kitty Chappell

A S I SAT on the patio enjoying a freshly brewed cup of coffee, a playful gust of wind swirled the fragrance from our rose garden around me, filling my nostrils with sweetness and my mind with bittersweet memories. It was Valentine's Day, and I shivered with fresh loneliness, aching for my husband, Jerry, who had passed away nine months earlier. Following a golf game, how he had loved sitting here with me drinking his favorite French Vanilla coffee — especially from this china.

Running my finger around the cup's delicate, 14-karat-gold rim, I again admired the beauty of the bright-colored roses gracing its sides, inside and out. I sighed deeply and took another slow sip. Leaning back in the patio chair, I recalled the many years I had dreamed of owning this set of Royal Albert Old Country Roses china but that was all I could do — dream. It was way out of our price range, as one dinner plate cost $100! I poured a fresh cup from the carafe and chuckled as I thought, had I played golf, I wouldn't now be enjoying this long-dreamed-of china.

I thought back to a time when I had timidly suggested to

Jerry how I felt somewhat resentful that he spent money on golfing, while I had no extra money for anything. "It's really not fair that just because I don't golf that I don't also get money to do fun things I want to do."

"Honey, you can buy anything you want, anytime you want it, and you can do anything you want. You know that," he chided softly.

"That's true," I admitted with a sigh, for I used the same checkbook as he. "But I feel frivolous if I spend money on things that I don't really need, and I don't have a sport that I enjoy. Besides, you know money sometimes is tight."

Pondering that for a moment, he asked gently, "Are you saying I shouldn't golf?"

"No, of course not," I replied. "You work hard, and you need to relax. You enjoy golfing more than anything else, and I would never want you to stop," I answered sincerely. I knew he always used coupons and rarely paid the full price for green fees, but inwardly I thought, "I work hard, too, putting in long evening hours at the hospital."

Jerry's friends had introduced him to golf right after we were married. That was the beginning of a love affair that lasted until his departure for heaven 47 years later. I smiled, remembering how he sometimes lovingly referred to me as his golf widow. I thought sadly, "Was it only nine months ago that I became his real widow?"

I cherished the memories of drinking coffee with him from these very cups following a golf game. As he excitedly replayed each stroke, I fought to keep my mind from wandering. I really didn't mind, though, for I treasured just listening to his voice as he talked about the sport he loved so dearly. Fortunately, my memory was never tested!

Several days following our conversation in which I had lamented my lack of spending money, Jerry said, "Sweetheart, I've been thinking about what you said and you are absolutely right! You too should have extra money to spend any way you want. Here's $25 for this month, and I'll give you that amount every month. Don't you dare spend it on groceries or bills or any necessities! And as our new business grows, I'll up the amount. That's only fair."

We both knew he didn't need to give me any money, but we both also knew I would never set any aside for myself.

I was thrilled. The problem was that having this extra money was so special that I didn't want to spend it. I decided to save it and wait until just the right treasure or event came along. Soon, my monthly allotment grew to $100. Each month when I received a crisp one hundred dollar bill, I added it to my cache, which I kept in a special place. I knew I should have put it in the bank; it would be safer there, but I wanted it near me, immediately accessible when the right occasion arose for its use.

One day I passed through the crowded china section of a department store and noticed a 50 percent off sign. With other things on my mind, I continued walking until I noticed a display of exquisite china, also 50 percent off. I stopped and stared. It was my long-forgotten-about dream china —Royal Albert Old Country Roses!

I ran home for my money and excitedly returned, praying, "God, please don't let all of my special china be gone."

I selected enough pieces to complete a service for six and tingled at the thought of surprising Jerry with my newfound treasure. "He is going to be SO excited!" I thought. Jerry also loved roses, and he had admired this china as much as I.

After a clerk took my china to the counter, I stood in a long line, my purse laden with cash. By the time I arrived at the cash register, the line behind me was even longer. When the young cashier glanced at my china, she sighed and confided, "I love this china and have wanted it for a long time. But I know I could never afford it."

I smiled and said, "Do you see these wrinkles, honey? Guess how long I have waited?"

After she rang everything up and announced the total, I began peeling off $100 bills. She exclaimed, "That's a lot of money!" The line behind me suddenly grew quiet.

"Yes it is," I answered, "and it has taken me a long time to save it. This is my golf money."

"You won all of this playing golf?" she gasped.

"Oh no," I said, "I received this from my husband for not playing golf!"

Murmurs ran through the line behind me. "Why didn't I think of that!" one woman grumbled. Another exclaimed, "What a great idea!" Several others said simultaneously, "Wait until I get home!"

When Jerry arrived home that evening, the china was displayed on the dining room table in all its beauty. In the center was a matching vase containing fresh cut fragrant roses from our garden. His expression was worth waiting for. He was elated and impressed. "You mean you saved all that money? I can't believe it!"

After that, Jerry surprised me on my birthdays, Valentine's Day and at Christmas with special pieces to complete my set. Thanks to his china gifts, my monthly golf money, and the annual half-price sales, my set grew to a complete service for twelve.

For over seven years, we enjoyed our china together. Even the simplest meal became elegant when served on the china and eaten by candlelight. I used it often. I had waited too long and wasn't about to save it for special occasions. Life is short and every day with my wonderful husband was a special occasion, made even more special because he had paid me not to play golf.

The Crying Lady in Atlanta Airport
The pay-off of trust

Joyce M. Saltman

Y EARS AGO, I had a speaking engagement in Atlanta, Georgia. Arriving on schedule, Kopi, my loving husband who died just three years ago, and I proceeded to the telephone carrel where we checked in to find out that our hotel did not offer shuttle service. Surprisingly, there was only one other person at the phones—a well-dressed woman, looking somewhat forlorn. Incapable of passing up an opportunity to connect with another human being, I approached the woman and asked, "Are you having a bad day?"

She responded, "I am having a *terrible* day! I was at a conference that ended a day early (something I never heard of in all the thousands of conferences I have attended over my 40 years of volunteer services) and all my friends were able to get earlier flights out, but I'm not leaving until tomorrow. Since I have only $20, I will have to stay here in the airport overnight."

"Well," I queried, "can't you call the conference people at the office to help you?"

"No," she replied. "They have all left."

"Don't you have a credit card?" I continued.

"Not with me", she responded.

"How about a checkbook?"

"No," she said, "I have nothing at all!"

I took out my wallet and insisted that she take $20 to be able to get a room in a motel near the airport. (In those days, Red Roof and comparable transient economy lodges were just $24 and $29 a night.) At first, she objected to a loan from a total stranger but I was finally able to convince the woman that anything was better than sleeping all night in the airport. She took my address, put the money in her wallet, thanked me profusely and left.

Kopi was somewhat taken aback by the entire transaction. He could not believe that I had given $20 to a complete stranger. He said I was too trusting and would probably never see the money again. When I asked why he hadn't stopped me, he said, "I was just relieved that you didn't invite her to stay in our room with us!" I must admit that the thought had crossed my mind, but I hadn't suggested it as our hotel was a distance from the airport and it seemed somewhat impractical.

A week later, having received no word from the lady in the airport, I reported the entire incident during a family dinner at my sister Teri's. My brother-in-law, who traveled constantly for business, told me that I had just fallen for the oldest scam in the world; at every airport in the United States, there are well-dressed people who have lost wallets or other such stories and without even requesting a cent, get unsuspecting, nice people like me to insist on them taking our money. My big brother said I had done the right thing, and Mom said, "Honey, if she doesn't return your $20, I'll split it with you so you'll only be out $10!"

Two weeks later, the check arrived with a lovely thank-you, thus proving the Feldman optimists correct. More importantly, a year later I received another note from the woman in the airport, reporting that she'd been through that same airport and this time she had a checkbook and a charge card, and the trip proved uneventful. She closed by saying that she thinks of me often and always says a little prayer that my life is going well.

And there it was—the thinnest of all possible threads! This was the reason that my life has been so bountifully blessed with good friends and kind deeds, joy-filled events and successes. Those little prayers that we don't even know about offered by the people we have offered a kind word to in passing, or listened to them when they needed an ear, are undoubtedly responsible for all the love that surrounds us. Those little prayers go directly into the universe, filling the world with positive energy, often directed at ourselves. The tiniest of good deeds have, indeed, made me the luckiest person in the world!

Habitat for Humanity

Katrina's gift

Becky Povich

> *"It takes hands to build a house, but*
> *only hearts can build a home."*
> -AUTHOR UNKNOWN

TARA RHODES' LIFE changed dramatically on August 29, 2005, the day Hurricane Katrina blustered into her life and the lives of countless others. The magnitude of the storm's fury left a physical aftermath of war-like destruction, and an emotional impact that would never completely fade away.

Before that ill-fated day, Tara's life was similar to that of many women. She was a single working mom with two young children and considered herself happy, in spite of struggling money-wise. She never really considered moving because she liked the climate, even though her soul kept feeling a persistent tug that God did not want her to be in Mississippi.

Two weeks after the hurricane, Tara was finally allowed to go back into her neighborhood and inspect her townhouse. What used to be her home was a shambles. She discovered one bright corner, though, which kept her from falling completely apart. Her "praying closet" was partially intact. That was the name she had given the walk-in closet in her bedroom. It was her private little haven where she kept a chair, her Bible and other essential documents. As she trudged toward it, she was utterly shocked to see that one side of the closet and its contents were soaked and damaged, but the side that contained those important papers and her chair was dry—including her Bible, still open and ready to provide words of comfort. Bible verses did console her for a while but, as time went by, she also couldn't help but ask the questions: "Why me, Lord? Why did this happen to me?"

During the next few months, Tara and her two children, Michael and Terrika, shuffled from place to place, which eventually brought them back home to Missouri. Although Tara believed she had already experienced her lowest possible state of mind, that didn't occur until the day she and her children walked into a homeless shelter in downtown St. Louis. She felt so humiliated and out of place as she observed the destitute and unkempt people surrounding her, many of whom suffered from mental illness or substance abuse. "We don't belong here," she thought to herself. As she waited for her number to be called, she held her children closer and promised their lives would soon be better, even though she barely believed it herself.

In early 2008, after two long years of living in substandard housing, one of her caseworkers suggested she apply for a home through HFHSCC (Habitat for Humanity St. Charles County), near St. Louis. The word was out that Habitat was looking for a family who had lost everything in Hurricane

Katrina. At first, she was excited. But soon she doubted the opportunity. She feared rejection and felt there must be some-one else who needed it as much as or more than she did. (Six months earlier, an unrelated agency had worked with her on a different housing opportunity that fell through, which just compounded her fears.)

Tara decided she couldn't give up and agreed to meet the people at Habitat for Humanity. The moment she walked into their office, she felt at ease and was comfortable discuss-ing her situation. Following the interview and paperwork, the only thing left to do was to wait. Patience, out of neces-sity, had become one of her best virtues. She tried not to get her hopes up since she had been disappointed so many times before. She didn't yearn for extravagance. She just wanted a nice home for her family in a good neighborhood. Was that too much to want? Four months later, Tara received informa-tion that would once again alter the course of her life; only this time, this life-changing moment was a positive one, a joyful one, a miraculous one! She knew she would never look at life quite the same way again.

She and her children were chosen to receive one of eight Habitat for Humanity houses to be built on a lovely cul-de-sac in a nice, family-friendly neighborhood! She could hardly believe it was true. For so long, all she had heard was "No. Not yet. I'm sorry." But this day was different. This was a day of celebration. The promise she made to her children at the homeless shelter so long ago was actually coming true.

When the time came for work to begin on her house, Tara threw herself into the "350 Sweat Equity Hours," meaning she, too, contributed to the building of her own home, which she considered an honor. The physical labor is part of Habitat's requirements of each home recipient. The owner must also pay a mortgage and insurance costs, contrary to widespread misconceptions about the organization's policies, one of which is that people receive a new house for free. This is simply not true!

In August 2008, Tara and her two children, who had been through so much, moved into their new home, almost three years to the day of losing everything they once had. Those long-ago possessions were no longer important to Tara as she realized her life was continuing on just the way it was meant to.

Footnote: July 2009. Tara loves her home and her life. In addition to working full-time and spending time with her children, she also teaches in a ministry and volunteers on behalf of Habitat for Humanity in St. Charles, helping others to realize their dreams of owning their own home. The quotation "God's grace is sufficient" is what kept Tara going during those very difficult years.

The Teacher Appears

Growing side by side

Kelly Seymour

THE OTHER KIDS called him Mochi, as in the mushy, traditional Japanese rice concoction. It sounds harmless enough, but what they meant was: Toshi's fat.

And he was. In a country where skinny is a birthright, Toshi Takaguchi stood out. He sat in the front row of my third-period English class, the one I'd come to dread teaching. Few kids paid attention; they preferred napping or drawing to vocabulary Bingo. The Japanese teachers were no help—they'd just shrug their shoulders and say, "It can't be helped." As for the kids, they thought of English the same way I thought of calculus: What's the point of learning something I'll never use? After almost a year in Japan, I realized that my dream of being the super teacher with a class of eager Japanese students was simply naive.

In class, Toshi usually slept. But sometimes I saw him watching me through the hair that splayed over his face as he cradled his head in his arms. It made me wonder—could there be a grain of interest in these students?

Every day after lunch there was a short cleaning period. Students would grab brooms, cloths and spray bottles, and do a reasonable job of tidying up the school. It was a fun, social time of the day, but it was also when I noticed Toshi being bullied. It seemed a daily ritual. "What did you eat for dinner, Mochi?" I heard someone yell once. Someone down the hall responded: "A pregnant pig and all her babies—with mayonnaise!" Toshi just pushed his mop from one end of the hall to the other, staring at the floor, always the floor.

I had taken to jogging every other day, something that garnered stares in rural Japan, but nonetheless it was a great stress reliever. It gave me time to think, and by the end of that year I needed it. It was coming time to renew my contract or return home, and I couldn't decide. While I enjoyed life in a different culture, I found myself missing people who understood me, missing being valued for anything other than my ability to speak English. After a year, I didn't feel a sense of accomplishment as I'd hoped; I didn't feel finished. I hadn't managed to teach much English and, though I'd been to the festivals and temples, I'd always felt more like the token foreigner than part of the community.

I was also disappointed in the school system. One afternoon after school I saw Toshi surrounded by a group of chanting kids. I couldn't understand their slang, but their tone and ugly expressions told me enough. For the first time, I lost my temper. I yelled at the mob. My words were incomprehensible to them (lucky for me) though my meaning was clear enough. The kids ran off and Toshi walked the other way, avoiding my eyes.

That night I ran hard to vent my anger. I watched the sun go down over a rice field and listened to the chorus of frogs, railing against the unfairness I'd witnessed.

Suddenly I heard footsteps beside me—Toshi!

"Hello," he said. He wore his school gym uniform: navy blue T-shirt and baggy sweats.

I followed my usual route, trying to pretend his presence was normal. Inside, I was panicking. Was he asking for help? How could I help him? After half a mile, when I could hear his labored breath behind me, I slowed to a walk. We didn't speak while we caught our breath; I felt awkward, embarrassed as a supposed authority figure, to try my so-so Japanese. When he was breathing more easily, I started jogging again. He followed silently, his shirt clinging to him front and back, not bothering to wipe the sweat that dripped over his eyebrows. When we were done, he bowed slightly and said, "Thank you." And then he turned and walked away.

He joined me almost every night, sweating and puffing without complaint. He followed me wherever I went.

I wish I could say that a few weeks was all Toshi needed to become slim and cool, to stop the teasing. It wasn't. But something about getting through to him, making some tangible difference in a world so foreign to me, did make a difference— to me. I decided to renew my contract and stay another year.

Over the course of that year I saw a change in Toshi. He ran with me often and even participated in the school's Sports Day. He won a fourth-place ribbon for the two-mile run. We began chatting on our runs, in English and Japanese. I was invited to dinner at his family's house a few times; his mother wrote a note on gilded stationery that said in the most formal Japanese, "We are indebted to you for changing the life of our eldest son."

The kids at school all knew about my befriending Toshi. Rather than turn them against me, it seemed to signal that I was human and capable of friendship. Word got out about my jogs and suddenly everyone wanted to come along. I started calling it "English Run"—anyone who wanted to could join as long as they conversed in English. Outside the classroom, the kids were relaxed, less afraid of making mistakes. When English became about connection rather than memorization, they were unstoppable. My second year in Japan flew by and I returned to the United States with no questions as to my future.

There's a Buddhist proverb I learned that year: "When the student is ready, the teacher appears." Years later, and still a teacher, I know that the reverse is just as true.

Don't You Love Me Dad?

Moving forward with hugs

Carol Sharpe

T HE PHONE SLAMMED hard against the shiny tabletop. "What do I have to do to please him?" Embarrassment caused Tom to hide his tears; he could hardly speak. This wasn't the first time this had happened. His dad's verbal abuse was constant.

Tom told me when we first met that his dad had shipped him off to the Navy as soon as he finished high school. "It will make a man out of you and put some sense in that head of yours." The brogue was still as thick as the day his dad left Scotland.

When Tom finished his stint in the Navy, he went to work for a successful business. Within two years he was made supervisor.

Tom rushed home and called his dad. "Guess what—I've been promoted, Dad. Isn't that great?"

"What the hell do you want now? I'm watching football and you're interrupting. No peace in my own home." The phone went silent.

The answer wasn't what he wanted to hear. Tom carefully placed the phone back and slowly walked away as his silence suffocated the empty room.

Five years later, Tom was promoted to upper management. He wanted to surprise his dad and would tell him at their regular Sunday dinner. His daughter, Suzie, and grandchildren would be there as well.

The atmosphere was tense. As usual, his father was in a sarcastic mood. Things never changed in Dave's house. He was the boss and his wife, June, was getting orders while running from the kitchen to the dining room.

The aroma of roast beef and oven-baked potatoes wafted throughout the rooms. His mom was a great cook, but Dave's favorite was roast beef so it was on the menu every Sunday.

No hugs or kisses were accepted in Dave's house. Anyone who was affectionate would be considered sneaky. Tom always wondered where that came from and his dad's vocabulary constantly consisted of racist slurs.

Cass, Tom's wife, couldn't believe that a man like that could have fathered Tom.

"Are you sure he's your real dad? You must take after your mom."

The table was set with June's best china. She loved to entertain but only had the chance on Sundays as they never socialized with anyone. She joined the church—not that she was religious, but it was an outing for her.

June carried the gravy bowl to the table and a bit of the liquid spotted the tablecloth. "June, can't you do anything right?" Dave yelled. His fist banged on the table, knocking over his wine glass.

"Clean up this bloody mess and hurry up!"

Cass bit her tongue as this man denigrated everyone.

There wasn't much conversation at the table. Attending every Sunday was for June's sake, and Tom's dad wouldn't eat anywhere else except at his "castle." When dinner was finished, Dave looked directly at Tom and threw his napkin on the table.

"So what's new?" he said in his usual surly voice.

"Dad, I've been promoted to general manager." The smile left Tom's face as quickly as it appeared.

"Well, it's about time you did something right. How long have you been with the company? Took you long enough. You should have worked harder; maybe you would have been promoted sooner."

The look on Tom's face made Cass feel ill; it was hard for her to hold back the tears. She didn't know whether to cry or lunge across the table at his dad.

"I'll be right back," Tom could hardly speak. He walked like a man 20 years older.

"June, bring my coffee and cake into the living room. I want to watch the news." This was said with no regard for Tom or the rest of the guests.

"What happened to 'Congratulation, my son, I'm proud of you?'" Cass stood up, stretched across the table and slung the words at his dad.

"What's there to say? So he got a promotion. It's about time he did something productive."

Cass couldn't contain herself any longer. She found Tom in the bathroom with his head cupped in his hands. She grabbed him by the arm.

"Get your coat, we're leaving this madhouse now!" The drive home was as quiet as the calm before the storm. Finally Tom said, "My own father doesn't love me. Why?"

"Tom, your father is a sick man. What kind of a childhood did he have?"

"He had a horrible time. Mom told me about the beatings with a razor strap everyday. My grandfather was sadistic to my grandmother, too. Dad ran away at the age of 15 and never looked back."

"Tom, you are a great father. It doesn't matter how tired you are. You always have time for the children. You attend their baseball, soccer and hockey games. Hoping to get your dad's approval is like going through a revolving door."

"Why do I let him treat me this way?" asked Tom. "He'll never love me the way he should. I've got to start acting like a man. He's out of my life for good."

A month later, June called Tom.

"Hi Tom, I have bad news for you."

"What's the matter with the old man now? What did I do wrong now?"

"It's nothing you did, Tom, it's your Dad. He's had a heart attack and a very bad one."

Tom grabbed the phone as it slipped from his hand. His head was reeling. His stomach was churning and he passed the phone over to Cass, trying to get composed.

His mom was still on the phone. Cass talked with June while Tom was still trying to think clearly.

"What the hell did you say to him?"

"His dad's had a heart attack. I don't think he's going to

make it."

"Sorry, Mom." Tim took the receiver from Cass.

"He's in the hospital. Do you want to see him?"

"Has he asked for me?"

"No, but I think you should come here."

They made it to the hospital and Cass stood outside the door while Tom was saying goodbye to a man whose approval used to be so important.

"Can I ask you a question?" His dad looked away.

"Why weren't you proud of me and why don't you love me?"

Dave lifted his oxygen mask and glared at Tom. There was a silence, and then his dad quietly said, "What do you want me to say? Do you need me to tell you how great you are? When will you ever grow up? I should have given you a few more licks like my dad did to me. Maybe that might have smartened you up."

Those were the last words Tom would ever hear from his father. The machine flatlined, the nurses scurried in and out of the room.

Tom looked back and whispered, "You are a pathetic man, Dad."

He stumbled towards Cass and held on tightly as if his whole world depended on this embrace. He held her face between his large soft hands.

"Let's go home to our wonderful children. I need to hug them." When they arrived, Tom gathered his children and looked into their beautiful faces. It startled them.

"Do you know how proud I am of you?" The heads bobbed

sideways and back like hand puppets not knowing what was to happen next.

"Well, I'm going to tell you I love you every day and how proud I am of you."

Tom laughed as the children toppled him to the floor with a group push.

He was true to his word. The children didn't have to go through life seeking the approval of strangers. Their father's blessing was there every day while encircled in their dad's arms. They didn't have to ask, "Don't you love me, Dad?"

Safari

Becoming my own person

Dorothy Stephens

WHEN MY HUSBAND burst through the door that September night in 1957, I had no idea how profoundly his news would change my life.

"We have our orders," he shouted. "A two-year tour of duty in Nairobi, Kenya!"

Nairobi? Wasn't that in Africa? What did he mean, two years in Nairobi, Kenya?

When Bob first joined the Foreign Service, I knew we'd eventually be sent overseas—to Paris, maybe? London? Rome? Nobody ever mentioned Africa. What little I knew about the "Dark Continent" came from the Tarzan movies of my childhood, and from the novel *Something of Value* by Robert Ruark. The book chronicled the bloody fight for independence called Mau Mau currently being waged by Kenya's Africans. I envisioned savage tribes, steaming jungles, ferocious wild animals and a host of tropical diseases.

"You don't expect me and the children to go there, do you?" I said.

But it turned out, he did.

"Don't worry," Bob said. "The Mau Mau rebellion is almost

over, and Nairobi is high and cool so malaria won't be a problem. We'll be fine!"

I looked around the dinner table at our children: Cathy, 11; Robbie, nine; and two-year-old Kelly in her highchair. Fine? I wanted to shout back at Bob. How could he think we'd be fine, taking our children to such a potentially dangerous place?

But I was raised during a time when a woman's role was to follow wherever her husband's career took him and to support him no matter what. I forced my fears into the back of my mind and set about the monumental task of moving a family of five overseas. I had just two months to see that we got all our shots and to shop for a two-year supply of clothes, shoes, footlockers and suitcases, Christmas and birthday gifts, toiletries and toys, and anything else we might need. There would be little available in Nairobi.

Somehow it all got done. In something of a daze, on a November night I climbed aboard the flight in New York that would take us to Rome. The following afternoon we took off again, this time in an old Air France Constellation, propellers thrashing and engines roaring, as it droned its way over Africa, 14 hours without seeing a light except for when we stopped to refuel at Tripoli's King Idris Airport.

When dawn came and the world finally reappeared, the Nile lay far below, a blue thread looping through the desert of southern Sudan. Soon, the Kenya highlands were sliding beneath us, vast farms that seemed to unroll for miles, and Kikuyu villages whose whitewashed houses and thatched roofs looked as neat as rows of beehives on the steep green ridges. A moment later, the wheels of the plane touched down. My encounter with Africa was about to begin.

My fears leaped back to life and bunched in a hard, cold knot in my stomach. Though the worst of Mau Mau was over, a state of emergency was still in effect. Jomo Kenyatta, alleged leader of Mau Mau, was being held in detention in the far north of Kenya, but the last remaining bands of rebels were still being hunted down in the forests and mountains outside of Nairobi.

I remembered with horror the story that had circulated recently through the State Department. A European child riding his tricycle near his home outside Nairobi had been attacked—and appallingly, unthinkably—beheaded by Mau Mau who sprang from the bushes wielding their *pangas*.

What were we doing here with three children? I wanted to turn around and fly straight home.

Our first few days in a Nairobi hotel were a blur of strange faces, unfamiliar foods in the Indian bazaar, streets full of sari-clad Indian women, African tribesmen wrapped in blankets, and African women in colorful lengths of cloth I would learn were called *kangas*. I saw only a few white faces.

When we moved into our rented house in the suburbs, four servants took over my roles of cook, housekeeper, gardener and laundress. I wandered around house and garden feeling lost and homesick.

But gradually I assumed other roles. Though I'd never done either before, I taught cooking to a class of African girls and swimming at my children's school. I became a Girl Guide captain, helped organize an international women's group that met for coffee in each other's homes, and entertained on a far more lavish scale than the neighborhood potlucks back home, often with visiting VIPs as our guests.

But the life-changing revelation came when I undertook a safari with the children—and without Bob. He was back in the States, having flown home when his father died and, in the sad days after we received the news, I pondered what to do. It was school vacation and we had reservations at a hotel in Malindi at the Coast. Nairobi was gray and cold, and the warm sun and sea of Malindi sounded tempting. Despite my misgivings about driving for 300 miles on a rough dirt road through empty bush full of big game, I decided to go.

We set off the following morning, after a "safari check" of the car. Leaving the city behind, we began the 300-mile descent to the coast. There were no signs of civilization, not even the occasional African village. I prayed we wouldn't meet any of the great game animals—lions, rhino or elephants—that inhabited this arid land.

We made a brief stop at a tiny British outpost for a snack of curried peas and warm orange squash, but after that we saw no other vehicles all day. What would I do, I wondered, if we ran out of gas? What if it got dark and no one came? My hands sweated in the heat, and blisters formed where I clutched the steering wheel. I felt as though we would go on traveling through Africa forever, pursuing some ephemeral African Shangri-la.

It was almost dusk when the dry plains gave way to coconut palms and banana trees, fanned by the trade winds and swaying amidst fields of sugar cane. The lush greens of trees and cane washed over me like cool rain, the vivid colors an assault on my eyes after hours of squinting through the dust.

As we rolled into Malindi a full moon rose out of the Indian Ocean. A kind of exultation filled me. For the first time I could remember, I had made a completely independent decision and had successfully carried it out. The turmoil of feminism was still somewhere in the future, but for me our safe arrival in Malindi was the beginning of my realization that I could be, wanted to be, not only a wife and mother, but that I was willing to take risks, try new things.

I didn't know it then, but I had taken the first step on a new path. I would go home at the end of our two years, enter graduate school and become a teacher and a freelance writer. Being in Africa had uncovered a core of independence and strength I hadn't known I had. This was Kenya's gift to me.

David's Story

The fulfillment of a wish

Denise Bar-Aharon

I HAD NEVER KNOWN anyone as generous and philanthropic as my brother, David Spero. On Thanksgiving Day, while still just a teen, David did not show up for our family dinners. Instead, he opened his compassionate heart and willing hands to be of service at our local soup kitchen, where the hungry gathered for their Thanksgiving Day meal. As a volunteer for Project Angel Food, David anonymously delivered food to the doorsteps of people suffering with AIDS. Had he lived longer, I know he would have continued on this path of service but, on January 5, 1994, David, age 29, died of cancer. His epitaph, "Born with a Kind and Giving Soul," was a testament to the life he lived, but it was not to be the only testament.

From the moment of diagnosis, we never gave up hope. So when his oncologist called and asked David to come in urgently—his blood count was elevated—we were all shocked. My father was horrified to receive the prognosis that it was likely his son had but six months left to live. With the weight of that news lying heavily upon me, I asked David if there was anything that he would like me to do in his name. He only smiled and said, "Just continue being good to others." While I was hoping for a more specific direction from him, I had to be content with that.

After he passed away, members of my family dreamed of him and felt him signaling his presence in the autumn air or in feathers falling at their feet. I, however, was given no sign even though David, in his last days, had promised me he would make his presence known to me if he could. I longed for that contact for two years, and then one night I had a dream that once again brought David and I together in a deep and profound way.

In the dream, he and I were in the children's fields of Kibbutz Rosh Hanikra in the north of Israel where we had lived as children. In this most beautiful spot on earth, David and I faced each other across a large ditch. There was a beam of light around his head and his hands extended toward me. I asked, "David, is that you?" and as the words left my lips I was lifted off my feet and into his arms. He said, "There is something I need you to do for me. Please help the children who are sick and dying." Still in his embrace, I called out "I'll do it!" and with that I awoke.

I told my husband and sister about the dream. "Where would I find these children that David spoke of? How could I help them?" I asked. They told me to just wait and keep my eyes and ears open, and that the answers would come. And they did.

The very next day at a friend's cocktail party, I was engaged in conversation with Mervin, a man literally bubbling over with excitement. He told me about his incredible experience as a volunteer "Pirate in the Caribbean" for the Make-A-Wish

Foundation.[*] Recalling the work of this foundation, I was dumbfounded. This was my signal from David. The Make-A-Wish Foundation is dedicated to helping children with life-threatening illnesses realize their final wishes. Mervin explained that he had wanted to start a Make-A-Wish affiliate in Israel but he was leaving the country in several months to take advantage of a business opportunity in the United States.

After speaking with my husband, Avi, we told Mervin that we would very much like to start an Israeli Make-A-Wish affiliate in my brother's honor. This was a wonderful way to fulfill David's last request of me, and also quite meaningful to me personally on another level. I knew that David was not able to realize his last wish to travel to India. Now, it seemed that by helping life-threatened children realize their last wishes, it would in some way satisfy David's last wish as well.

Now 15 years later, Make-A-Wish Israel has granted more than 1,500 wishes to Israeli children—both Jews and Arabs. The foundation has not only enriched the lives of these sick children, but has also enriched the lives of hundreds of volunteers from elementary schools, Israeli Scouts and the military. Today I am proud to serve on the board of directors of Make-A-Wish International. The experience continues to touch me and enrich me as I help to make these children's dreams come true. While I cannot add days to the children's lives, I can certainly add life to their days and, in so doing, David's kind and giving soul lives on.

School for Wonder

Arriving just in time

Jesse White

E LAINE HEDGES WAS my first women's studies professor at Towson University in 1982. She was a renowned
scholar on the history of women's quilts and a pioneer in
bringing women's studies into academia for the first time in
history. She was noted in *Who's Who*, which I had never heard
of when I met her.

I enrolled in her Culture and Creativity class my first semester in college. I was so taken by Elaine and her elegant style of
teaching that I took big risks and shared with her the poems I
had secretly been writing to my women friends. I was amazed
that a teacher actually wanted to be my friend. We met in her
office, my heart pounding and her eyes twinkling. The first
book of poetry she loaned me was *I Am Not Your Laughing
Daughter* by her friend, Ellen Bass.

My final assignment was to teach her class, and I covered
the history of female friendship. I devoured the material, and
talked about female leaders as though I knew them personally. I was probably overflowing with passion more than I was
actually teaching. I couldn't believe there was a forum for
friendship in a college-level class.

When the hour was over Elaine and I walked outside together. Her jade eyes practically bloomed in the sun. She shook her head at me, and I trembled in fear that maybe I had done it all wrong. I can still remember holding my breath, my hand on a railing to steady me, waiting for her to speak.

She looked right into my eyes and said, "In all my years in the classroom I've never seen anyone be more comfortable teaching. If only I could do what you do. You're a natural-born teacher!"

That moment changed the course of my life. It was as though she had handed me a baton and sent me off as an advocate for female friendship, as well as for being a teacher who didn't need a degree.

I quit college at the end of that semester, and the search for my own curriculum began. She elevated me above her academic colleagues who had training but no gift. Big-headed and foolish, I decided to leave the university. I thought I didn't need a degree.

Elaine cried when I sat opposite her smooth wooden desk and told her I would be leaving school, traveling for a year or two, and landing in the Southwest. Her eyes filled to the brim and she whispered, "I will miss you so much. You have no idea how much you mean to me, how rare students like you really are in this place."

She invited me to her Roland Park home in Baltimore to say goodbye, where I realized we were from very different worlds. I climbed the front steps of the elegant old house dressed in loose white muslin trousers and sandals, carrying a small gift. The box I held was handmade of beveled glass, crafted especially for me by a woman friend, with irises etched into the glass lid and a mirror in the bottom. I asked her not to open it until I returned, and clarified by saying, "I'll be back to open it with you when I know who I am." She looked puzzled, but didn't question me.

My plan was to come back and open the box with her when I had created something worthy of my own to give her. With Elaine in mind, many years later I designed a book in a box, on unbound poem cards, so each one could be displayed individually. The box had a spine just like a book, and I registered it in the Library of Congress. In my own mind, I was not worthy of anything until I had contributed something of merit to the written world.

I wrote her a letter after my book was published in 1996, about how unexplainable our connection had been for me, and how she had shown me to myself so clearly. I told her how the School for Wonder had come into being, partly because of what she taught me. I wanted to reflect back how she had inspired me, mentored me silently for all those years.

I had written her many letters during my 15-year absence, but never had the courage to send a single one until then. Elaine was the mentor I pressed my soul against, and the archetype I never quite lived up to in my own mind. I had secretly wished many times that I could return to her late in life and be there when she died. It felt monumental to finally write the beloved letter that would bring her back into my life, and I cried as I wrote it.

I telephoned the college in Maryland where Elaine and I met, and they said she was away at her New England cottage. I mailed the book along with the letter I had written with great care. I told her how much my love had grown for her during the long silence, and how it shaped me to live my way toward the creative dream and finally open the sacred box with her.

When I mailed the letter and the book I felt like a young kid again, anxiously waiting to hear her response after first teaching her class 14 years earlier. A week after I posted the letter and book, I got a call from Elaine's best friend in New York. Choking back tears, she said, "Your book and letter made it to Elaine's mailbox the day before she died!"

Elaine never saw the letter or book, but our connection was so strong it thrilled me to know I had been present at the time of her death, if only in her mailbox. Elaine's friend asked if she could read my letter and a poem from my book in a box, *Dominion of Wings*, at the funeral.

Elaine's best friend shouldered my grief in that phone call exactly as Elaine would have wanted it: warmly, with dignity and quietly.

Making a Difference

Sharing and caring for soles

Greg Woodburn

I N HIS FAMOUS poem *The Road Not Taken,* Robert Frost
noted: "Two roads diverged in a wood, and I/ I took the
one less traveled by, and that has made all the difference."

When I was eight years old, I began traveling on a sports
"road" less traveled. Instead of football, basketball or baseball,
I diverged off the well-worn path and chose an oval "road"
lined with eight lanes; I joined a local youth track team and
that has made all the difference.

Distance races are the ones I love. I thrive on the challenge of flying one mile or two miles on the track, or three
miles through the woods in cross-country races. I enjoy the
discipline and dedication that goes into training, and the
camaraderie I have developed in running—and laughing—
with teammates. Most of all, I relish testing myself in races.

As a youth runner, I earned many individual ribbons, tro-
phies and even team medals at national championship meets.
Ironically, while my triumphs on the track have been memorable, my disasters have been in many ways more rewarding.
And make no mistake, I have experienced hard times. Indeed,

the early success I enjoyed came to a crashing halt my freshman year in high school; my ambitious goals and dreams were replaced with a stress fracture in my left hip. As a sophomore, disappointment struck again in the form of serious knee problems. At the time, I could not have been more devastated.

Today, however, I consider those injuries true blessings. You see, while I was sidelined I fully realized how deeply I love the sport of running and all it has given me, such as confidence and self-esteem, dedication skills, improved health and friendships. I was certain I would eventually get healthy and be able to run and race again, but I started thinking about those who cannot enjoy this great sport and its many benefits—not because of injury, but simply because they cannot afford running shoes.

So it was that I turned a negative force into a positive one by creating Give Running, my own nonprofit organization dedicated to giving running shoes to underprivileged youth. My initial goal was 100 pairs of running shoes. By spreading the word about my project and placing collection boxes at local schools, gyms and running stores, I topped 100 pairs and kept going. I topped 1,000 and didn't stop. Instead, I sped up! To date, I have personally collected, scrubbed by hand, and donated more than 2,100 pairs of refurbished running shoes. And I have no plans to slow down.

Give Running not only greatly exceeded my expectations in terms of numbers. I have been able to distribute the shoes to more places than I dared think possible—near and far, from inner-city Los Angeles to Mexico to Sudan, Uganda and Kenya in Africa. The feedback from youths in Africa has been especially touching. Not only are these the first running shoes any of them have owned, they are the first shoes of any kind most of them have ever had.

I have adopted a quotation—and core belief, really—from legendary basketball coach John Wooden as Give Running's motto: "There is great joy in doing something for somebody else." This truly summarizes what I have learned from my Give Running endeavor. There are so many wonderful and generous people who want to aid others, but sometimes they simply don't know how to help. I am proud to help show them a worthy avenue. While Give Running aims to aid underprivileged youth, I have found that the adults and children who donate shoes also get great joy out of contributing.

People assume scrubbing the dirty, smelly shoes would be a gross chore, but the truth is that when I'm toiling away at the sink I actually find myself smiling because I imagine the smile of the kid when he or she receives the shoes and laces them up and goes out for a run. While scrubbing away, I often think about a quotation I read by the late Jacqueline Kennedy Onassis, who once observed: "One man can make a difference and every man should try."

I'm trying to make a difference in my own small way, one shoe and one person at a time. As a constant reminder to keep trying to make a difference, I have taped Onassis' words of inspiration to my bathroom mirror, right alongside Give Running's motto from Coach Wooden. In addition, here is another quote I have taped to my mirror. It's from Wayne Bryan, the father of professional tennis superstars and super role models, Mike and Bob: "If you don't make an effort to help those who are less fortunate than you are, well then you're just wasting your life."

I don't want to waste my life.

Also adorning my mirror is a thoughtful hand-written note from American distance record holder and 2004 Olympic marathon bronze medalist, Deena Kastor, who has become a huge supporter of the Give Running program: "Greg—continue making a positive difference in all you do!"

Deena's words inspire me daily. I don't want to let her down.

Here is one more quotation taped to my VERY crowded mirror—luckily I have a buzz haircut and don't have to see myself to comb my hair! This one is from Hall of Fame baseball manager Sparky Anderson: "Character is doing what's right when no one is looking."

Actually, someone is always looking at me figuratively— me! And I don't want to let me down by not being a person of high character. I want to positively impact the world as a person of the highest character, as someone who wants to shrink the world and bring people together, who is blind to religion and race and only sees fellow human beings.

Among my many aspirations, I dream of one day running Give Running full time to impact as many people as possible. I also want to coach track and cross country at the high school level so I can positively affect local youth.

Maybe I can even inspire them the way Coach Wooden, Deena Kastor, and Mike and Bob Bryan have inspired me. Maybe one day a kid will even tape one of my quotations to his or her bathroom mirror!

I am now healthy and excited about chasing this many racing goals in college. But my ultimate running dream does not involve prestigious medals or epic championships. My dream is to one day be in a race—maybe in college, maybe at the Boston Marathon, maybe at a local 5K—with one of the kids from Africa or Mexico who got interested in running thanks to a pair of shoes I collected, cleaned and sent his or her way. That would be true affirmation that I have "made all the difference." I get goose bumps just imagining it.

Broken Pieces

Holding on to what matters most

Sylvia Skrmetta

L ATER I WOULD wonder what made me take that last photograph of my home. I was running late. The rest of my street had already been evacuated, and I needed to report to the hospital before the streets became impassable.

I had volunteered to replace one of the other nurses who needed to get her young family out of town. My grown children and their families had been given direct orders from me earlier that day. "You need to leave," I told each of them. "It's going to get bad."

Luckily, they recognized the urgency in my voice and did not argue. My husband was reluctant to leave me, but I had begged him to pick up my elderly parents in Biloxi and drive to Atlanta where we had family.

The hospital was a torrent of activity. We were in an emergency situation, and only hospital personnel with proper identification were allowed in the building. Doctors, nurses and ancillary staff flooded the halls. Each carried whatever they deemed necessary to weather the storm and the following days and nights. We were the "On Team."

Hurricane Katrina hit the Mississippi Gulf Coast without

mercy for life or property. Each nurse was acutely aware
that his or her own family was out there — either staying in
the area after moving to higher ground on their way to safe
havens; or, hopefully, already safely out of harm's way.

Landlines and cell phones no longer worked as the unfalter-
ing winds and rain pummeled the coastline. Lights flickered
in the hospital, but soon we were plunged into total darkness.
Emergency generators kicked on within seconds, and sighs of
gratitude emerged from us all. Luckily, we were an outpatient
unit and there were no patients with whom to be concerned.
Then again, if we had been busy with patients, we would
not have been so aware of the glass breaking in the adjacent
hallway and the force of the wind pulling the walls apart just
outside of our door.

Rainwater began to steadily stream under the door and
into the unit. We had been instructed to save all clean linens
for use after the storm, so we were forced to grab bags of dirty
hospital laundry from the storerooms to ebb the flow. Alarms
sounded throughout the hospital building. Windows in the
upstairs patient units were blowing out or shattering. Despite
the fact that our building was coming apart little by little,
several of our nurses made their way upstairs to help move
patients out of their rooms and into the hallways. The rest of
us were instructed to keep our unit as secure as possible, for
we would soon be receiving the victims of the storm.

Hours went by. Would it ever end? The normally chatty
group of co-workers, who had prattled through the first few
hours, had become silent in thought and prayer. The storm
had been so violent and had lasted so long that most of us

knew the worst was yet to come.

Soon we could hear people on the other side of our unit door. We had not been aware that the debris from the disintegrated hallway had us trapped. Immediately, the nurses were given orders to report to the emergency room to help triage incoming storm victims.

For several hours, we waited as the emergency vehicles and personnel precariously inched their way to victims and then back to the hospital. Finally, the deluge began. Besides the visibly wounded brought in by the emergency crews, scores of wet and battered people began to emerge. There was emptiness in their eyes and desperation on their faces that simply outweighed any physical injury they may have endured.

Doctors and nurses — some of them in cut-off jeans, shorts and T-shirts — attended to the injured. Many patients had no identification, and some were so confused that it was nearly impossible to get pertinent information from them. Those who could talk did so nonstop. Everyone had a story and wanted someone to listen.

I knew my house was gone when I heard the reports from the emergency crews, but I still hoped for a miracle. It was almost a week later before my entire family returned home, and we made our way to our property.

I stood in the exact same spot I had taken the photograph more than a week before. However, this time I was photographing a slab with mountains of debris all around it that included possessions from homes on neighboring streets.

Somewhere between what used to be my kitchen and dining room, I stood motionless, mesmerized over my excellent taste in flooring which somehow had remained intact. I was totally oblivious to the huge crocodile tears streaming down my grown daughters' cheeks as they stared at me with sympathetic eyes. This had been our dream home; the home we had waited 30 years to build. I imagine they must have thought their mother would erupt in hysteria or fall to her knees in a blubbering spectacle. Surprisingly, I became excited as the sunlight reflected on an object partially buried in the muck. With the enthusiasm of an archeologist on a monumental quest, I jumped off my slab into the sea of slime left behind by the storm surge and embarked on the treasure hunt of my life. My family followed suit. Each member found a spot to search around the foundation. With their hands and feet covered in slimy mud, they dug. Every time some minuscule item was uncovered, the family cheered and ultimately elevated and glorified the find to the equivalence of discovering King Tut's tomb.

Several exhausting hours later, a rather grubby, smelly family marveled at the odd collection of treasures that had been left behind and lovingly recovered after the worst hurricane to hit the United States. Half a dozen plastic containers, deposited on our property by the storm, now contained the broken pieces of what was left of 40 years of our lives.

Now it was my turn to gaze at my incredible family. They were a dirty, wonderful bunch of wonder. I could always accumulate new stuff, junk or whatever a human calls the endless parade of items one feels is necessary to pad a nest. Knowing my plate was cleared — that my life was turned upside down and inside out and we were still going to be OK — was somewhat of a surprising revelation. I could replace the things taken by the storm, but I could never replace my family — the kind of family that gets on their hands and knees to dig in filthy, slimy, stinky mud to find meaningless "crap." Nothing could ever take that away from me.

Rekindler of the Light
May Sarton, my muse

Deborah Straw

"I AM SIMPLY AMAZED at all you do for people," my mentor wrote me 20 summers ago. "But now there must come a way to do some writing of your own."

Each time we spoke, May repeated similar words. She praised my efforts and related her experiences.

And here I am. Writing.

To earn a living, I still teach writing and literature to adult students three days a week. I am often exhausted after grading papers and devising lesson plans. It isn't easy to find the psychic energy or time to do my writing. I have lots of excuses—washing dishes, walking the dog, unloading the laundry, reading my favorite authors.

Out of necessity, as I approached and passed 40, I summoned the strength to change some of my non-productive writing habits. Maybe I'd enroll in an MFA program. Or maybe I'd look for a mentor, an experienced writer who could advise me about the world of literature. Of course, I wanted to find just the right one, someone whose work I admired.

And then, out of the blue, the choice was made clear for me. From a bookseller's tip, I learned my favorite writer, May

Sarton, was to sign books in my town. I found out the date, sent May an invitation to dinner, and the rest is history. She came, we ate chicken and salad and drank Scotch, and we hit it off. Thus began our intense relationship.

Since that first meeting, we met every two or three months, sometimes at her suggestion, many at mine. I gladly drove four hours back and forth from Vermont to her oceanside home in Maine to share her company for two hours or the occasional overnight. Each time, she was an inspiring conversationalist, enthusiastic about my writing endeavors.

We began with niceties (weather talk, discussion about birds or our cats) and a cup of tea on her screened porch, but almost right away, she wanted to know what I was writing. She uttered a hearty "Bravo!" when I took a new risk. I tried many genres—poetry, personal essay, short fiction—and she encouraged me to experiment. She recommended books by authors, particularly women, she considered fine or unusual— Virginia Woolf, Ruth Pitter, Barbara Kingsolver. She loaned me their work and gave me her own.

We also discussed her projects—her frustrations, deadlines and recent reviews, both praising and damning. She talked of relationships, past and present, with editors, agents, readers and critics, and she related stories of her early mentors and friends—Virginia Woolf, Elizabeth Bowen, Hilda Doolittle (known as H.D.)—thrilling names from a glorious past literary world.

Although May didn't read all my manuscripts, she consistently offered encouragement, ideas for markets, and positive feedback on a title or topic. When she did read something, she was cautiously positive and firmly critical. She told me one or two things she liked very much—a word here, an image there—and one or two things she thought needed work. For example, although she appreciated an essay's thesis and the quotes I chose, she felt the work was repetitious. It was hard to hear her negative criticism, but I knew it was good for me. It's what I do for my students; they can take it. May's suggestions were generally spot-on.

Between our visits, when she wasn't immersed in a manuscript, she wrote me wonderful letters. Like her books, they were graciously worded, about nature, friends, books and, of course, ideas. Not coincidentally, many of my interests and literary themes—France, writers, women's friendship, cats— were similar to hers. I resisted imitation.

Until I established this connection, I didn't have a clear idea of what having a mentor involved. I can now say it seemed like magic. It kept me in a high state of excitement, nourished and intrigued. May was part role model, part mother and part friend. She delighted and fascinated and scared me. I was full of renewed energy each time we spoke.

Since meeting this woman, my life has changed enormously, particularly in my ability to write more. I have made the transition from repeating others' thoughts (I have been a successful journalist for 30 years) to expressing my own. I write or revise nearly every day.

This month, I sent a short story in to a literary journal and three poems to a competition. I am writing essays and sending them out on spec to national magazines. My mentor even, at times, became my muse. She appears here and in a few poems.

I've learned to revise more effectively, away from my house and its demands.

Because May wrote poetry, I pay more attention to contemporary poets. I attend readings and am not afraid to speak to nationally prominent writers about their work and lives. In my writing classes, I use poetry to show the importance of choosing precise words and images. And I'm writing my own poems. Suddenly, poetry is an essential part of my life.

Finally, I took steps to ensure I keep writing. About 15 years ago, I started a writers' group of published women writers, and our Sunday evening meetings have become a highlight of my life. They provide an informal deadline and a discipline I haven't always had. But the group and its process are daunting. Last week, when I received some pointed comments about an ending and lack of adequate conflict in a story, I felt like quitting. Creative writing is a lonely business and harder work than I had expected.

Of course, my personality hasn't changed. I still do too much for others. But the help I offer seems to have increased in quality. I have protégés of my own.

Terry, 20, came into my English Composition class with a weak vocabulary and unfocused ideas. She watched too much TV and read too few books. After two semesters, she was writing tight, mature essays about the importance of her elderly dog and art in her daily life.

Sally, 94, began writing in my group at an adult day care center at age 92. Drawing on a rich life of travel, two husbands, children and grandchildren, she began to get up in the middle of the night to jot down her thoughts. She noticed every bird and the way moonlight cast shadows on her apartment's walls.

These things might never have happened if I had not met May Sarton. Even when I didn't speak to or see her for weeks, just thinking about her commitment, her talent and her belief in me always pulled me back on track.

Albert Schweitzer, a mentor I never met, wrote, "Sometimes our light goes out but is blown again into flame by an encounter with another human being. Each of us owes the deepest thanks to those who have rekindled this inner light."

His words help me comprehend some of the spark that existed between May and me. I don't know how I got along without my mentor, but I'm glad she helped me rekindle my light when it was flickering. And as she taught me, I keep passing the light along.

Mother by Proxy
A true model for motherhood

Kathryn Rothschadl

M Y RELATIONSHIP WITH my mother did not begin in the usual way. I was not born of her womb. Her blood does not course through my veins and I didn't inherit her soft green eyes or her slender frame. Nor was I the result of someone else's poor planning, later to be adopted by my mother. She became my mother by proxy.

She came into my life at a time when I truly needed a mother. At first I resented her, even disrespected her. I saw her as an intruder on my life and I wanted nothing to do with her. But my opinion of her changed one hot summer afternoon. She brought me a glass of ice water as I was playing in the yard. I began to gulp it down and unwittingly inhaled a large ice cube. It became lodged in my throat and I began to panic. My mother saw my distress and immediately ran to my aid. She helped to dislodge the ice cube and then pulled me into a gentle embrace as I cried. All my resentment for her immediately disappeared and at that moment I knew that she was truly my mother.

Throughout my childhood, we did the kinds of things mothers and daughters are supposed to do. We went shopping, did errands, read books and watched movies together. She taught me how to cook and clean, tend the garden and do household chores. She savored little moments with me—times when it was just the two of us and we could do something special. Money was always tight, but she found creative ways for us to have fun. She was strict but fair and I adored her.

When I was a teenager, we had the usual ups and downs that girls and their mothers have. We fought and made up. I hated her and loved her. I pushed her away and always came back to her. She encouraged me to join extracurricular groups at school and to pursue a college degree. She reminded me of how difficult it had been for her to earn her degree so much later in life. And when I finally went off to college, we both experienced a loneliness we never anticipated. Somehow, through all the ups and downs, triumphs and tragedies, she was no longer just my mother; she had become my best friend.

Today as an adult, I am forever grateful that this woman who did not give birth to me, who did not adopt me, and who had not planned on having me in her life, has given so much of herself for me. She is the one I call when I've had a bad day. She's the one I long for when I'm sick in bed. She is the one who can comfort me, reassure me and support me when I need it most.

Now that I have children of my own, I know how strong and how beautiful the bond is between a mother and her children. I understand the responsibility to put my children before myself. I ache when they hurt and I smile when they are happy. But could I so unselfishly provide for and love a child who was not my own? I would like to think so. I would like to think I have learned through example.

As I watch her with my own children now, I am amazed at her patience and understanding. I am touched by how deeply she loves them and reminded of how blessed I am that she came into my life. Had our paths never crossed, I have no doubt that I would not be the person I am today. My life most certainly would have disintegrated into a downward spiral. The moment she entered my life, she changed the path I would take. She steered me in the right direction and stayed with me until she was certain I wouldn't lose my way. Then she entrusted me to continue on my own, and became a beacon in the distance, a presence to let me know she was always there if I needed her.

My mother does not fit the negative stereotypes associated with her role. She was never cruel to me. She never put her birth children before me. She has given me nothing but unconditional love.

She is the single most influential person in my life. She is my stepmother and I am proud to call this beautiful woman "Mom."

Santa's Helper Was a State Trooper

Reaching in and reaching out

Linda O'Connell

MANY CHRISTMASES HAVE passed since I opened the door to a uniformed Alaska state trooper.

By 3 p.m. it was pitch dark; every single star in the sky seemed as bright as the Star of Bethlehem that December day in 1969. I was pregnant with my first baby, living at the top of the world, literally, and missing my mom more than ever. I couldn't believe how close and bright the stars appeared in the Alaska wilderness town where my former husband, a soldier, and I were assigned for nearly two years. Wild animals roamed down our gravel road and into the nearby woods. Often a small herd of buffaloes thundered past; I glimpsed the antlers of a moose or a reindeer loping by. Once I came face to face with a buffalo and her calf. We all froze in our tracks, wide eyes illuminated only by starlight. I softly murmured, "Don't worry; your baby's going to be OK." I was talking to myself as I clutched my belly and backed myself indoors.

Christmas was two weeks away, and the temperature was minus 40 degrees. We'd chopped down a five-foot evergreen from the small forest across the road. It stood bare in the living room for nearly a week as I waited impatiently for my mom to mail my Christmas ornaments. Each day around mid-morning, I pulled my long johns over my big belly and tugged on two pairs of pants, socks and my insulated boots. I wriggled into my dark blue furry parka and headed up the snow-covered foot path that led to the rural post office in the tiny town located at the end of the Alaska Highway. The biting wind froze my eyelashes; my exhaled breath came out in tiny ice crystal clouds.

I despised the winter darkness; I wanted to sleep day and night. Daylight was no brighter than a dim light bulb. I felt sorry for myself, deprived of all the things I wanted like fruits; I craved watermelon like most pregnant women crave ice cream. I needed vegetables, but most of all, I wanted my mom. I wanted to place her hand on my belly when the baby kicked. I wanted to sit down and dunk a donut with her and talk about the baby, but mom and "home" seemed a million miles away.

When the elderly postmistress handed me my package, I smiled broadly and wished her a Merry Christmas. I clutched the box to my chest possessively, imagining each of my Christmas ornaments inside. I wandered through the general store, wished through the maternity clothes and baby items and warmed myself thoroughly before heading back out into the bitter wind. I hurried home to open my package. I discovered an envelope along with my decorations. I ripped it open, and five crisp one-dollar bills fell out of the card. It seemed like a fortune. As tempted as I was, and as desperately as I wanted to hear my mom's voice, I knew I shouldn't convert the money to quarters to feed the pay phone and make a long-distance

call. I decided I would instead mail a "thank you." After deco-
rating the tree, I sat down and wrote a long letter, then instead
of napping as usual I headed back to the post office. I was
prepared to buy the things we needed and wanted: stamps
and a carton of milk, which was exorbitantly expensive. I'd
buy fruit, the same fruits that I found each Christmas in my
stocking when I was a child: apples and oranges. What I really
wanted, though, was a slice of sweet, juicy watermelon to satisfy my craving. Where could I possibly get watermelon in the
middle of winter in the Arctic?

I had been home only a few minutes when our next-door
neighbors knocked. My best friend's husband held his hands
behind his back. "I have a surprise for you." He grinned like a
little boy with a secret. He extended his unwrapped offering,
and I almost gagged. I forced a smile and examined the jar of
pickled watermelon rind.

"I know you've been craving watermelon," he said.

"Thank you." What else could I say?

When he left, I felt so lonely. I turned to look at the decorated tree, which reminded me of my hometown. In my mind,
I reached for my mother's comforting hug.

Within the hour there was an insistent knock on the door.
My heart hammered as the Alaska state trooper asked my
name. He handed me a written message that read, *Call your
mother immediately.* I imagined a tragedy.

"We don't have a telephone or money for the pay phone,"
I admitted, having spent the five dollars. The trooper said he
was acquainted with the retired school teachers who lived at
the end of our road. "They have a telephone; tell them I said

it's OK." I was as embarrassed as I was worried. I dialed the rotary dial with a shaky hand.

"Mom, it's me; are you OK?" My voice quivered.

"Yes. I didn't know how to reach you any other way. You don't have a phone, or a street address, only a post office box, so I told the kind officer that you lived in the green trailer on the school road. I just had to talk to my girl and tell the little mother merry Christmas."

I breathed an audible sigh. I wanted to sink into the carpet on my knees and rejoice. Walking home in the dark, I realized that reaching for someone is much different than extending a hand to someone. While I was brooding, selfishly reaching *for* specific foods and my mother, others reached out *to* me. Kind neighbors allowed me to use their telephone. I heard Mom's voice when I needed it most; and my well-intentioned friend gifted me with pickled watermelon.

Thereafter, I made it a practice to reach out to other lonely soldiers' wives who needed a cup of sugar, a word of praise or a helping hand. Like those unbelievably close and brilliant stars that lit up our nights in Alaska, one gesture of kindness sparked another as a dozen of us young, expectant mothers reached out to one another and briefly illuminated each other's lives.

The Million Dollar Deal
The power of a family story

Lucien Padawer

WINSTON CHURCHILL SAVED England with words and my father saved my business with words as well. Let me tell you the story.

My father immigrated to Paris from a small "shteitle" in Poland, taking with him only "a propos" stories told him by his grandfather. Soon after arriving he met my mother and they later married.

At a time when the only modes of transportation for workers and farmers were bicycles or walking, a new French invention—rubberized cotton fabric which made it rainproof —made my father seize an opportunity. He and my mother moved to Belgium where it rains 300 days a year. He rented a brownstone with a storefront on the main street of Liege, set up a workshop on the second floor and living quarters on the third.

He was all set. He just could not meet the demand for the waterproof hooded capes he produced, covering bicyclists and pedestrians from head to toe and at last, keeping them dry.

This was the right idea at the right time in the right place. Three years later, he opened a factory in Brussels with 100 workers, established 69 stores throughout the country and built the house where I was born in 1928.

Life was a dream until May 1940 when Hitler's Germany invaded Belgium.

During the next year my father had to share the administration of the business with the nephew of the German general in charge of Belgium. The house was sold at a fraction of the cost, money was gathered from loyal store managers and, in April 1941, the family escaped Belgium on one hour's notice after having been warned of imminent arrest. We landed in New York Harbor in June 1942.

At the end of the war, my father recovered the business and in 1947, on my first visit to Belgium during New York University's summer recess, I mixed vacation with a search for how to finance my high-maintenance social life as a 19-year-old student. I imported trench coats produced in our factory (now in water-repellent finish) and had them distributed in the United States through a rainwear business run by a college friend's father. The proceeds were sufficient to finance my needs at the time.

After graduating, my goal was to make the trench coat as popular as were Hush Puppies with coeds and as the London Fog balmacaan was for millions of Americans. If London Fog could have their balmacaan in every U.S. department store, my firm, Foxrun, could do the same. And so it was. Every department store and chain in the United States was selling the "Foxrun Trench." I was the king of the trench coat.

Life was a dream until two years later, when it became a nightmare.

By then, I was in charge of the Belgian business and had expanded production to meet the American demand. We were employing hundreds of workers producing trench coats and made two mills in Flanders very rich. They could barely weave the fabric fast enough to meet our orders.

On a warm humid day in July, as I was sitting at my desk in my office on the 38th floor of a Seventh Avenue skyscraper, the switchboard rang. "The Bloomingdale's buyer is on the phone" announced the receptionist. Anticipating another reorder, I happily took the call.

"Hello Jack."

"Hi Lucien. You better come over right away. We have problems."

I arrived at the store on 59th Street, rushing to the rainwear department. On the way up the escalator, I smelled an unpleasant odor. As I approached the rainwear department, the odor became stronger.

Jack greeted me with a worried look on his face.

"Lucien, the air conditioner intake is directly over your raincoats and the whole store smells of fish."

As I put my nose to a raincoat, I thought I smelled a *dead* fish.

I suddenly recalled that a few days earlier, just before one of my salesmen was to meet with the Neiman Marcus coat buyer in Dallas, he had a Foxrun trench coat pressed at a nearby dry cleaner. Standing next to the steam press, as the coat was being processed, he detected a strong odor of fish. He called me from the dry cleaner and I immediately telexed our manager in Brussels: "Howard in Dallas just called. Had a Trench Coat steam pressed. Coat smells from fish. Investigate."

The response, which I will never forget, was: "Press Howard, see how he smells." (Belgium never experiences the heat and humidity we do in many parts of the United States.) At the time I dismissed the response and considered it amusing, if not a bit sarcastic. I did not anticipate the events that followed. We later discovered that the mills, in order to save time and pennies, skipped the "wash after" process required to "fix" the formaldehyde application of the water repellency finish.

Thousands of trench coats were coming back from all over the United States as the summer humidity brought out the fish odor in our raincoats. We tried experimenting with all available methods to remove the smell with ammonia fumes. We set up a "shack" in a small empty loft next to our showroom and had a "Mr. Bloe," who represented himself as an expert deodorizer, treat a rack of our coats. Within an hour after beginning the process, an elevator operator came to my office and said: "The whole building smells from ammonia and everyone is crying." The deodorizing operation had to stop and was resumed at night.

The first rack came out of the "shack." We rented huge fans to air the coats. We then sent the rack to Bloomingdale's and waited anxiously for Jack's call.

The call came and the news was not good.

I asked: "Is the fish smell gone"

Jack replied: "Yes ... but it now smells from piss!"

I had a disaster on my hands. Our bank, which financed the invoices for merchandise shipped, was now going to be exposed to more than a one million dollar loss as the returned defective merchandise was no longer payable.

I decided to preempt the unavoidable confrontation with Lou, the bank's president. After calling him and telling him that I needed to see him urgently, I went to his office.

We sat in the conference room. Lou liked me and in prior years I had occasion to quote some of my father's stories, which he always enjoyed. When we first met I was in my early 30s and Lou was something of a father figure to me.

I went into detail, explaining what was happening and mentioned that I intended to hold the mills accountable. I assured him that we were now producing trench coats without smell and would replace the returned coats. I also shared with him the drama surrounding the unexpected visit from the woman who catapulted into my office, bypassing everyone in the reception area and showroom, throwing herself at me screaming "SMELL ME! SMELL ME! They made me get off the subway at 42nd Street and told me to go take a shower!" I thought this might reduce the tension.

Silence followed. Lou was absorbing the news and did not look happy. After a moment we had the following exchange:

Lou: "Well, what do you have in mind? This is very serious."

Me: "I am convinced that with your help I can turn this around."

Lou: "How? And what help?"

Me: "Well, with an additional bridge loan for one million dollars, giving us time to deliver the replacement coats."

Lou looked at me incredulously.

"As much as I would like to advance you the money," he

said, "first I have to account to the bank. Second, you do not have the additional collateral we would normally need. And third, I have a partner with whom I need to consult."

I smiled.

"I am turning you down and you smile?" he said.

"You remind me of one of my father's stories," I replied.

"Which one?" he asked.

"This man came to his friend and asked him to give him back the pot he had loaned him. The friend replied by saying: 'First, you did not lend me any pot; second, I gave it back to you; and third, it is broken!'"

Complete silence followed. I knew that Lou was in a position to grant me the loan and had the authority to do so. I also knew that he had to consider the choice of having me turn the situation around and save my company as well as the bank's investment or, if he turned me down, the bank would lose not only the unpaid invoices but also other loans covered by my company's line of credit. As well, I would be out of business. Yet if he granted the loan and I failed, it would increase their loss by an additional million. I could feel my heart pounding.

After a long pause, Lou smiled and said, "I like that story. You got your million!"

Foxrun grew into the leading trend-setting outerwear company in the United States for many years until it was sold. Lou had made the right decision.

My father's stories came in handy many times in my life. Without this one, how could I have responded to the turn-down? Life is full of coincidences and how lucky I was to own that story when I desperately needed it.

Waiting for our Miracle

Prevailing against all odds

Perry P. Perkins

WHEN I WAS a boy, my mother had a small plaque that hung in the kitchen of our tiny apartment.

It read, "Even miracles take a little time."

My wife and I had planned on being the typical American couple. We would marry, work for a couple of years (to earn some stability and get to know one another) and then start our family. We had seen our friends follow this same agenda and it seemed simple enough.

We learned it was not always so simple.

There were years of self-doubt, frustration and bittersweet smiles as we held the newborn babies of our closest friends, all the while agonizing over the empty place in our own home and hearts, the frustration of not being able to give each other the baby we wanted so badly, while longing to be the parents that we knew God had made us to be.

Finally, after a decade of trying and reaching the ripe old age of 38, we realized that having a baby just wasn't going to happen the "old-fashioned way."

So we sought help.

Only we found that "help" is expensive; "help" is very

expensive. The process of IVF (in vitro fertilization) and a subsequent pregnancy and birth would cost tens of thousands of dollars. We had $300 in the bank.

It was a long night at the dinner table. There was anger and there were tears. How could God put such a burning desire, such a lifelong goal to be parents in our hearts, and then make it impossible to achieve?

We didn't have tens of thousands of dollars; we didn't have $1,000. But we did have our house.

Years of scrimping and saving, driving clunker cars and brown-bagging lunches had allowed us to pay off our school debts and save just enough for a down payment on a beautiful little three-bedroom, two-bath house on the outskirts of town.

We had waited and worked hard for our miracle.

Vickie and I both worked full-time, living in tiny apartments in bad neighborhoods to save money, crunching numbers until they squeaked and jumping though every hoop imaginable for 10 years to buy that house. It wasn't much, but it was ours. For a kid who'd never lived anywhere but apartment complexes, it was everything. A place to have friends over, plant our own flowers and paint the walls whatever shade of purple we pleased—a place of our own. It had been like a dream come true when, three years before, we'd signed papers and moved in, and now it was being made clear to us:

We could have our baby—if we gave up our home.

The market was ripe and our agent assured us that we could get our asking price, which would leave us just enough to pay off our loan and our few remaining debts, and complete the

IVF process one time.

We talked. We argued. We cried.

Most of all, we prayed.

That's when we realized that everything we had scrimped and saved and sacrificed for had been leading to this moment. We weren't being forced out of our home; we were being given an opportunity to have the child we'd always wanted—and all we had to trade for our miracle baby was this block of brick and stone.

People all over the world suffered through childless lives, and we had been given a blank check. A check with three bedrooms, two baths, and a garage—all we had to do was sign it.

And we did.

More sacrifices were made, possessions were sold, and more tears were shed when we stood in the living room of yet another tiny two-bedroom apartment. Then the innumerable trips to the doctor, the embarrassing medical tests, the extremely candid conversations with nurses, and the seemingly unending "are we" or "aren't we" months of limbo, hope and heartbreak.

During the IVF appointment, only four viable eggs were found. On the morning of implantation, only one had survived. Our doctor put it to us straight: the odds were long against us but, as he put it, "We're here anyway, if you want to give it a try."

We knew we couldn't afford another treatment. We knew we needed a miracle. So, we prayed and cried and said yes. Then, once again, we waited.

It's been four years since we sold our dream house, and our

daughter Grace just turned two. Nothing about her addition to our family was easy; not her conception, her birth, or her first weeks at home, but she has brought light to our lives that no windows could, and colors to our world that no flowers can ever match—she is truly our miracle baby.

Sometimes we talk about how we miss our house, and we look at pictures of our brief time there and feel a little sad.

Then baby Gracie smiles and laughs and hugs our necks and we know that sometimes miracles take a little time; sometimes they require a sacrifice, and that our miracle was worth both.

True Passion

The musical moments that changed me

Sandra Freeman

MY HOUSE WAS always filled with the sound of music. My mother was a torch singer during World War II, and my father was a happy whistler of any new, popular tune. I, however, fell in love with classical music. The love affair started early and, by the age of five, I was able to sound out any song on the piano that I heard.

I had a thirst to learn more and to become better able to play the intricate pieces of the masters. Consequently, my piano lessons lasted all through my college years. I was fortunate to have wonderfully inspiring teachers who only increased my love for the art.

One such teacher took it upon herself to give me an extra push into performance art. In sixth grade, she enrolled me in the New York State competition for classical music.

I was excited, yet frightened to death that I would not be good enough. I would be competing with students much older than me and from all over the state. However, my teacher believed in me and said, despite my age, I was performing at the same level of musical competency as the other entrants.

I practiced day and night, for I was determined to win the

championship. Even as I lay in my bed at night, I imagined my fingers flying over the piano keys. The sweet music I heard in my head lulled me to sleep each night.

The day finally arrived and, as I sat excitedly waiting for my name to be called, I readied myself for my debut. "Sandra Shapiro," the announcer called. I floated to the performing platform, unaware of anyone and anything except the piano on the stage. I sat down and performed *Solfegietto* by Richard McClanahan by heart and from my heart. It was just me and this magnificent concert grand piano, an instrument upon which I had previously never played.

When the piece was finished, I knew inside that I had done well. Soon, I heard my name announced again. This time it was to award me the first-place ribbon in the competition. The joy I felt was unsurpassable, but more importantly I knew this was a turning point in my young life. At the tender age of 11, I had been granted an epiphany. I had found my passion and I would follow it all my life. Who knew where it would lead and what part it would play in my life? What I did know is that my world had been radically changed and that I would always hear music playing in the background of the scenes of my life.

Although through the years and life's many changes I lost track of that special award ribbon, my love of music remained, as well as the confidence that was instilled in me by winning the competition. That triumph gave me the strength through-out my life to branch out and try things I never thought I could do.

I did not pursue a performance career in music, but the

piano always gave me comfort and allowed me to comfort others. Many years later, I found myself working at a total care senior rest home as a music recreational counselor. Upon reading the biographies of my patients, I discovered that one woman was a very well-touted piano teacher. In fact, my best friend of 25 years had taken piano lessons from her! It was she who had introduced him to all the great classical piano venues of Europe and had encouraged him in his career. He had lost touch with her and was now able to reconnect.

Unfortunately, this woman's mind was quite deteriorated through dementia. She never spoke, and there was no indication that she could even hear or comprehend what was said to her. Her world was small, as her life was lived in a wheelchair that was lined up against the wall with her co-patients.

To break the monotony, one day I carefully wheeled her over to the piano in the recreation room. I gently placed her hands on the piano keys. This woman, who showed no response to any stimuli whatsoever and who had to be fed and physically cared for, began playing, in perfect repose, a piece by Amadeus Mozart.

Despite her physical afflictions, the music still resided deep inside of her. It was entwined in her soul, as it is entwined in mine. Without a semblance of rationality, this woman "remembered" the beauty of Mozart's work and shared a special moment with me. Her muscle memory allowed her to play the pieces that were so deeply ingrained, and I was honored to be her only and final audience.

We can never lose our true passion. It is ours forever. In my times of crisis and despair, I often remember this incident. It soothes my soul, gives me hope and inspires me to move forward. It reminds me to never let go of my passion, for it will continue to surprise me as I travel along my path of life.

Stitch by Stitch

Spreading kindness all year long

Dallas Woodburn

LINDSAY BAXTER, A 17-year-old high school junior from Laguna Niguel, California, was taught to knit when she was 12 by two of her close friends. "I like learning new things and knitting seemed like a fun and practical craft," she says. A versatile athlete—she enjoys playing soccer, tennis, basketball, running and swimming—Lindsay found knitting to be a calming contrast to her physically active endeavors. It gives her time to sit quietly and clear her head. She knits scarves, beanies and blankets, and after giving away her creations as presents to friends and family, she began accumulating many knitted items that, she says, "I had no use for."

When she traveled to New York and Chicago during the winter months, Lindsay was surprised and alarmed to see how many disadvantaged children and their families had to face the frigid weather without warm winter gear. It was nearing Christmas, a time of hope and giving, yet still there were people sleeping outside on the sidewalks during the freezing nights. "I realized I could use my knitting skills to give warmth to these people in need," Lindsay says.

Upon returning home, she gathered up her knitted

creations and took them to Skid Row in Los Angeles to hand out as gifts to homeless people. "I went a couple of days before Christmas," Lindsay explains, "and there was some kind of hand-out going on in a local church for needy people in the area. There were so many people in need there and they were so excited to get a scarf or beanie." She was amazed by the genuine gratitude and appreciation people had upon receiving the scarves and beanies she had made. Lindsay says, "I decided I wanted to try to get more people involved and make an even bigger impact." So she started Knit with Love, an organization that provides scarves, caps, blankets and other knitted items to people in need.

Lindsay built a website, www.knitwithlove.org, to spread the word about her endeavors and try to get others involved—even those who don't know how to knit. Her website's homepage encourages knitters to join the effort, while also inviting non-knitters to get involved by donating yarn and other knitting supplies to the organization. "Help us put a smile on a deserving person's face today!" Lindsay writes on her website. Knitting, she believes, can be a means of inspiring people to come together for a common cause. She regularly receives packages of donated knitted items from volunteers across the country. As Knit with Love grows, Lindsay hopes people will form knitting groups and host knitting drives in their hometowns.

"My favorite part about volunteering to help others," Lindsay says, "is seeing the joy and excitement that something I have knitted can bring to a person. It is so great that a single item can make such an impact on people."

Knitting is a fun activity to begin with. But Lindsay believes that when you are knitting a scarf or a beanie that is going to someone in need it becomes a much more fulfilling endeavor. The Knit with Love website states, "Every item we knit is knit with love and with a specific purpose in mind. Our goal is to provide warmth, hope and love to people in need." To be sure, the scarves and beanies Lindsay donates are more cherished because they are handmade; the recipients can feel the love that went into every stitch.

Knit with Love has now grown to 15 active members from all over the United States. Recent projects include donating small beanies to children undergoing cancer treatments at the Children's Hospital of Orange County; giving scarves to children and their parents at a homeless shelter in Los Angeles; and sending a box of knitted items to a shelter in Seattle, Washington. Knit with Love also frequently sends donations to StandUp for Kids, an organization that works with homeless shelters across the nation.

"Through the donations I have also been able to see how easy it is to make a difference in someone's life," Lindsay says. "I have learned that there are a lot of people in the world who are less fortunate than I am. I've grown a much greater appreciation for my blessings—my family, where I live and my lifestyle in general."

Lindsay's future plans include going to college to get a good education, and then finding a job she loves, possibly in a health field such as physical therapy or nutrition. In addition, she says she hopes to continue to grow Knit with Love "to reach more people and impact more lives."

Indeed, Knit with Love has already touched a great many lives. It is evident that Lindsay is passionate about brightening the lives of others through knitting. How can other young people find community service projects they enjoy? Lindsay advises, "People should strive to find something they love doing and then find a way to use that to benefit others." She emphasizes that volunteering to help others doesn't feel like work because it brings her so much happiness. "Helping others is a very rewarding feeling," she says.

For such an active, driven, busy girl, time must be precious. When asked where she finds her inspiration, Lindsay says, "I think we are meant to help others in whatever way we can. For me, that is knitting scarves and beanies to brighten the lives of homeless and sick people." Many people participate in toy drives or food drives during Christmastime and experience the joy of giving. Through Knit with Love, Lindsay perpetuates this joy and selflessness all year long.

To get involved with Knit with Love, you can e-mail Lindsay at info@knitwithlove.org or go to her website, www.knitwithlove.org, for more information.

Fly Little Bird, Fly!

The story of a mother letting go

Erika Hoffman

WHEN MY DAUGHTER, Heather, told me her plans for spring break during her sophomore year at University of North Carolina at Chapel Hill, I said, "Sounds dangerous." My daughter's idea to sign up with Medical Ministry International and trek to the jungles of Ecuador, where she'd travel on big canoes with outboard motors along the Napo River from village to village, dispensing medicines and treatments to folks whose church pews serve as examining tables for the itinerant doctors, dentists, and nurses of MMI, was not my idea of what spring break should be.

Before leaving, she had to receive inoculations: hepatitis A, tetanus, yellow fever and typhoid. She needed a prescription for malaria pills and altitude pills. She got a flu shot. Since she'd already been administered the series of hepatitis B shots in her local public school in sixth grade, she checked one requirement off. Arranging inoculations wasn't simple, quick or cheap. My friends at exercise class asked, "Are you sure you want her to go through that?"

Heather fainted during administration of the yellow fever shot. Her arm swelled up; she became nauseated the next day and slept through her classes. "It may be an omen; maybe she shouldn't go," my friends cautioned.

Packing was nightmarish. MMI asks its volunteers for medical supplies: 50 pounds worth in one suitcase. The other suitcase is for personal belongings. Though last minute, we scrambled and secured 50 pounds worth of antibiotics and medical supplies; then we filled up half of her personal bag with toothbrushes and paste. The inventory list should have been mailed to customs in Ecuador months before the trip, but we had only three days left before she embarked. "Customs may not let her through, and the inventory must be typed up on a special document," the director instructed. Most meds were obtained from her dad's practice and a local pharmacist. Our dentist donated an inexhaustible pile of toothbrushes and paste. We prayed Customs would let her through with this munificence.

As the days dwindled away before her trip, she drove home more often. She needed to study for her organic chemistry 2 exam as well as complete a myriad of presentations and labs, also due before spring recess. Her broom closet room at her sorority house on Rosemary Street didn't lend itself to spreading out notes and cramming. With the passing of each day leading up to spring break, my daughter became a walking zombie. She pulled all nighters.

"Wouldn't she rather go to Florida for spring break?" my buddy asked.

"A *Girls Gone Wild*-type of vacation?" I queried.

"Aren't you worried about South American jungles?" another added.

"Bad things can happen to good girls on break at the beach. I saw *Where the Boys Are*," I said. Although I answered my pals' concerns breezily, I wasn't certain I believed my flip answers.

During the days before spring break '08, fighting broke out along the border between Columbia and Venezuela. The United States sided with Columbia, while Ecuador backed Chavez of Venezuela.

"Did you see the news? Shouldn't you cancel your daughter's trip?" probed my friends.

Two days before her flight, I took my daughter shopping at Super Target for comfortable clothes that qualified as modest and disposable. She packed her suitcases to the brim. I stayed up Wednesday night typing the inventory list of medical donations while she crammed for her organic chemistry test scheduled for Friday morning at 8 a.m., hours before her noon departure. I faxed the list and crossed my fingers.

Wednesday night, I learned that Heather's friend decided not to accompany her on the return trip, but instead planned on spending a second week in the jungle. This meant my daughter had to journey alone on a public bus for five hours to Quito, locate and check into a hotel, and catch a taxi at 4 a.m. to make her 6:40 a.m. return flight to Miami.

"Mom, I have to get back Saturday night to study Sunday before classes start up. It'll be OK. Nothing bad will happen."

"Out of the question!" I told her. "I won't sleep a bit worrying about you all alone, trying to navigate your way to a strange airport with limited schoolgirl Spanish in a South American country with a high crime rate."

I seized the phone, praying a seat existed for her on a flight that next Sunday, the day following her booked ticket. On that Sunday, she could travel in the company of the dentists from MMI who would also be returning home.

On Thursday morning, March 6, the day before her departure, I succeeded in switching Heather's return ticket, paying another $340 for the exchange. Now she'd arrive with a group and leave with a group. I believe there is safety in numbers. I could sleep.

Thursday afternoon she returned home to study. Reading at a table near her and her spread-out papers, I jumped when the jangling phone startled us. "I can't talk now. No time. Really. I have to go," she explained to her boyfriend as she fidgeted with numerous notes and graphs. "What?" she said. "No!" Her voice softened to a whisper. "How horrible," she uttered. I perked up. Her hands jumped to her mouth covering it. "That's so sad." Her eyes darted. She pressed them closed. "I will be careful. Thanks for calling." She put the receiver in the cradle slowly. She fell into the chair, stunned. "Mom, something terrible has happened! Our student body president has been shot to death a mile from campus. They found her body lying on a slope of a hill, in a neighborhood, just left there. They didn't even know who she was at first." Her eyes explored mine.

We watched TV. Carolina Parents sent us an e-mail alert. Another pal phoned with more details. Eve Carson's cottage was a stone's throw from my daughter's sorority house. From where my daughter parked her car, one could see little Friendly Lane, where Eve was living and studying in her residence the night she was abducted, robbed and murdered.

My daughter's professor postponed the chemistry exam. A campus was in a meltdown. How could this happen to the best, the brightest, the beautiful and beloved Eve? All who knew her echoed the same refrain—a wonderful, caring, exemplary person. This was the life stolen that warm spring night for an ATM card. An innocent victim of an untimely, cruel and savage demise. A daughter snatched while studying on her couch. A good girl. A student with promise. A leader who cared for those less fortunate and less gifted. Why?

I put my daughter on the plane the next day for Ecuador. Her sorority sister joined her after all on the same flight; she changed her ticket to return with her as well.

"Vaya con Dios; Go with God," I whispered to my sweet girl.

I read in Philippians: Do not worry about anything, but pray and ask God for everything you need, always giving thanks.

We cannot take the future for granted or dwell on the past. Our children are in God's hands; we must let them fly from the nest no matter how much we worry about the unknown. Who can judge where they will be safe and where they won't? Going to a foreign land surrounded by poverty, disease and political unrest can ironically and sadly be safer than one's own couch in a calm university town. All we can do is put our trust in God, our faith in tomorrow, and give our love away.

Five Little Words

A surprise twin blessing

Harriet Hodgson

THE SOUND OF the ringing phone was jarring. When I answered it, my granddaughter cried, "Grandma, there's been another car crash. Daddy is hurt and the dog is hurt."

"Grandpa and I will be right over," I soothed.

My husband and I had already received more than our share of sad news. In February of 2007 our elder daughter died from the injuries she received in a car crash. Two days later my father-in-law succumbed to pneumonia. I sobbed uncontrollably when I saw their photos on the same page of the newspaper.

My daughter's former husband offered to move into the house with our twin grandchildren and live with them until they graduated from high school. We accepted his offer. Things were going pretty well and then, two months later, my brother died of a heart attack.

Now, another life hung in the balance.

As we drove to the twins' house, a terrible thought came to mind. What would we do if the twins' father died? I didn't share this thought with my husband, yet my mind was racing. We picked up the twins and drove to the hospital emergency room.

I became suspicious when the security guard asked for our name and directed us to a section of the waiting area. Something was terribly, terribly wrong. A nurse escorted us through double doors and down a long hallway to a small waiting room. My son-in-law's sister met us at the door. "Did you hear the news?" she asked.

"No," I answered anxiously.

"Jim died," she said. The twins' eyes widened in shock, and they wailed in grief. I could barely hold myself together.

"Why is this happening to us?" my granddaughter asked.

The youth minister and other relatives arrived. A pall of sorrow hung over the room and few words were spoken. After the doctor gave his final report, we still sat there. Stunned. Since our daughter had listed us as the twins' guardians in her will, I turned to them and said, "You're coming home with us."

I knew these words—five little words—would change my life. This was more than a defining moment, it was a sacred moment. Though I'm a strong person and have good coping skills, I was scared. Could I parent teens again? Would I have enough energy? What about my writing career?

We stopped by the house again so the twins could pick up some clothes. As soon as we returned home, they went to bed, each in their own rooms. My new life had begun. How had it changed?

Five words have given me a new reason for living. Protecting and providing for my grandchildren is my life mission. My husband and I were used to changing our plans quickly. Today, our plans revolve around the twins' schedules. We tried to stay in touch with friends, but have come to realize we're out of step.

Friends tell stories about the cruises and tours they have taken. We tell stories about band concerts, choir concerts, gymnastics meets, potluck suppers and sleepovers. Three years into the grief journey, we continue to provide a loving and nurturing home for the children we love so much. The twins have become "our kids."

Both of them are outstanding students and members of the National Honor Society. They share their feelings with us and their conversations include "our" and "we" and "home," all ownership words. Witnessing their college search has been fun and, though they haven't yet chosen their careers, we have launched them into adulthood. When the twins leave for college, we will be empty-nesters again. I will miss the sound of running feet, booming rock music and teenage laughter. I will miss hearing them ask, "Grandma, what's for dinner?"

Five words changed my life forever, and I am blessed.

The Angel and the Butterfly

Not a fly-by visit

Lorri Danzig

H E HAD BEEN my mentor for 20 years. A spiritual master and a brilliant Renaissance man, he had tutored me in the ways of the sacred and the ways of the ordinary. With his guidance I had undergone a metamorphosis. Once an earthbound caterpillar, I had emerged as a butterfly. When he died, I was overwhelmed by grief and apprehension. I feared that with his death I would plummet back into my spiritually impoverished life as a caterpillar. Weighted down by both despair and a carry-on, I made my way through Kahului Airport. I would soon be soaring at 30,000 feet and, while the plane would carry me into the heavens, I did not anticipate any encounters with angels.

In the days before 9/11 forever changed the world, taking an inter-island flight was like taking a bus. There were no seat assignments; just hand over your ticket and grab a seat for the short hop to a neighboring island. The boarding line for the next flight to Oahu was very long. I was standing at the middle of the line, daydreaming and people-watching, when a slight and haggard woman approached me dragging a carpetbag.

"I can't stand for very long so I'd like to board as soon as possible. Would you mind if I cut in front of you?" she asked.

"No, of course not," I said, eyeing her as I took a step back to allow her in line. She was gaunt and bird-like, all jutting bones and sharp edges. Her dull, black hair hung down her back in a scraggly mess of split ends. The dark circles under her eyes and the greenish tinge to her translucent skin gave her a ghostly appearance. Why, I wondered, had she approached me? Why hadn't she gone right to the front of the line with her request? Anyone could see she wasn't well. These unanswered questions hovered as the boarding line began its shuffle forward.

I offered to carry her bag and was surprised by its weight as I hoisted it over my shoulder. "Why don't we find two seats together?" I said. "Then I can help you with your bag again when we land." She thanked me as we made our way onto the tarmac and boarded the plane.

We sat together in unbroken silence as the doors closed and the flight attendant recited the safety instructions. It was shortly after takeoff when she turned to me and without ceremony unraveled the tale of her 10-year struggle with breast cancer. Now metastasized to her bones, it had caused numerous hairline fractures and a broken clavicle. This, she explained, was why she had been dragging the bag behind her.

"Despite the metastasis and the pain," she said, "I feel more well now then I have ever felt in my life. I have a spiritual teacher. He is a medical doctor. He couldn't cure me, but he did guide me to a place of deep healing within myself. I finally feel whole."

With that she fell quiet again. I was stunned by her unsolicited personal disclosure and marveled at the coincidence. She, too, had a spiritual teacher. She, too, felt blessed by his influence on her life. After a long pause, she began to speak again, softly but with great strength.

"I feel that you are grieving. And despairing," she said.

I stared back at her, dumbstruck and rattled. How could she know this? I'd told her nothing about myself. Was I so transparent?

I hesitated only a moment before opening up to her. "Yes, you're right. I also had a teacher. He passed away two months ago and I'm having a hard time sorting through the implications of his death. I wonder how much of what I learned from him is really mine; how much will die with him."

She did not respond right away, but seemed to be studying me, reading my doubts like tea leaves.

"His teaching is now part of you. It will not die with him. With it you can continue your journey on your own and it's important that you do. Your dependence upon his guidance became a limitation. His death freed you so you could continue to grow."

She turned her head away from me and closed her eyes as salty rivulets of relief and gratitude rolled down my cheeks. My lungs inflated with hope. The corset of tension constricting my chest split at the seams. I stared out at the night sky and felt my teacher's wink in every flickering star.

After deplaning, she and I walked together to her connecting gate.

"I want you to have this recording of a talk given by my teacher," she said when we arrived. "Just promise me that if it's not of value to you that you will pass it on to someone else."

Thanking her, I bent down to tuck the cassette into my own bag. As I straightened back up, I found myself standing alone. There was no sign of her. I looked for her in the gate area but she was gone. How was that possible? She moved so slowly dragging her bag and I had only looked down for a moment. What was her name? I could not remember. Had she even told me? She had appeared and then disappeared, leaving behind her words of encouragement like nectar for a butterfly. She left me with the strength and the courage to test my wings. She left me believing in angels.

A Selfless Thought

The power of a parting message

T HE CALL CAME at 2:30 that afternoon; it was my
brother Brian. He rarely called me at work, so I was curious about the nature of the call. I looked forward to a brief
respite from the suffocating heat and humidity. Working in a
steel mill during the summer can be close to unbearable. My
feet felt like bags of concrete as I plodded up the stairs to the
air-conditioned control room to answer the phone.

"Tom, it's Brian. Dad is real sick and he's at Duke University
Hospital. You should call Donna and come down as soon as
possible." Hanging up the phone, I thought, "What? Dad
sick? My tough-as-nails Marine Corps father? Not possible!"

The next few hours were a frenzied blur of booking flights,
packing and calling my sister Donna. My father had confided
in Donna that he had not been feeling well for some time.
But, as was his nature, he toughed things out and seldom went
to a doctor. He had told Donna his appetite was off and he
felt nauseous at times. Nursing was her profession so of course
she advised him to get checked out. But he wouldn't.

After losing 25 pounds and no longer able to take the pain,
Dad went to the doctor. After a series of scans and tests, his

158

doctor told him, "You have no choice; you have to go to the best hospital you can find."

It had been many years since most of the family had been together. There are eight of us, four boys and four girls. Careers and spouses had dispersed us many miles apart and it was difficult to get us all together; however, this was an event that would. I guess there is some truth that births, weddings, sickness and funerals bring families together.

Donna and I were like old friends and we chatted the entire trip down to North Carolina. But it was mainly mindless small talk; we were simply avoiding the topic we knew we must eventually address. Stepping off the plane in North Carolina and into the stifling 96-degree heat and high humidity, along with the din of airplane noise, reminded me of my job back home.

We gathered our luggage and were shuttled to our hotel. We sat in a hard-to-break silence, as if there was an impending doom. No sooner had I placed my bags in the room then my cell phone chirped. "I'll pick you up in 10 minutes," brother Brian said. "Meet me out front."

He broke the news on the way to the hospital. My father was in the oncology unit and my heart sank because I knew what that meant. As I glanced at Donna, her bottom lip quivered and she looked out the window as tears welled up in her eyes.

As we walked across the street to Duke Medical Center, I was aware of the traffic but didn't hear it. My senses felt as if they were in partial shut-down mode.

In the oncology unit I embraced my siblings and

half-heartedly listened to the doctor as he briefed us in a counseling room. He described Dad's conditions, the progression and nature of the cancer. All I wanted to do was see my dad.

My mother was in the room with my dad; four of my siblings went in to see him. "He can't be sick. He looks too good," I thought. But I knew better. I hugged him hello and in hindsight it was the only time I had ever done so. After a few minutes he said, "I want to see Tom and Donna alone."

We spoke of his chances of beating the cancer, options such as chemo treatments or an operation. According to his doctor nothing really held much promise for him. The cancer had entwined itself so deeply in and around the pancreas that to operate would be pointless.

Suddenly Dad lurched forward and he broke down. Crying, he said, "I don't care what they do, just no more pain!" My mom hugged him around the neck and buried her head in his shoulder. Dad turned his head toward hers and their sobs were the only sound I heard. They had recently celebrated 50 years of marriage, but today they knew they wouldn't reach another anniversary date.

I had endured a rocky marriage for years and it was no secret to the family. After regaining his composure, Dad asked me, "How are things at home?"

"Well, you know the way she is," I replied. My wife, although a good homemaker, had a volatile and unpredictable temper.

"We always thought she took a good deal of your love away from us, Tom. Don't prolong things; do what you have to do to be happy. Take care of yourself and your sons."

I touched his hand, not knowing what to say. My tough Marine Corps Dad, always fit and trim, fitting into his World War II uniform until his death. He knows he's going to die and he's thinking of me, I thought.

That was the last time I saw or spoke to my father. I called a few times, but he was too weak to talk on the phone. My sister Mary took her new son, Andrew, to see him in October of 1998. They made a video of Dad holding baby Andrew. My dad was there on video but he wasn't; he had a haunting stare that pains me to this day. There was only the shell of the man that I had known, feared, loved and respected. He was a survivor of a major war, having fought in a pivotal battle that killed and maimed many men. He was physically and emotionally tough and was now in a battle he could not win. If it were in his power to fight back, he would have. Only now he was being subjected to the insult of being consumed from within.

Chester J. Adessa passed away November 3, 1998, just a few days before his 78th birthday. His selfless words in the hospital that day changed my life. Although it took some time, I ended my toxic marriage and found happiness with another woman. The relationships with my sons have also been altered. Sometimes my oldest son, Chris, 29, calls me four times a day. I look at life through simpler eyes now and focus on big pleasures from little events. Although my wife and I walk in a nearby park nearly every day, there is always something new to enjoy. On Thanksgiving I always prepare the stuffing and turkey the way my father did. When I make my father's version of spaghetti sauce I remember how he would sit at the kitchen island and talk with my sons. Dad wasn't a knowledgeable wine person, but he would enjoy any new wine I introduced him to. Over a recent glass of Syrah I wonder how he would have liked the peppery finish and smokiness of a particular vintage.

In many conversations with my sons I have told them that in 10 seconds you can alter your life forever. In August of 1998 that happened to me. In just a few seconds, with a few words, a dying man changed my life.

Middle School Miracle
Students are often our best teachers

Michele Rae Eich

M Y EIGHTH GRADE class was in the midst of preparing for the culminating activity of the year: Outward Ingersoll, a three-day education program held every May in the great outdoors. As the outing approached, I could feel the tension rising among my students. I waited for someone to ask the dreaded question: What about Ronny?

Ronny was a sweet kid who always had something friendly to say. I marveled at his positive attitude despite the overwhelming challenges he faced in his young life. Middle school can be a brutal place to navigate the tumultuous years of adolescence, a place where kids can be unkind and even cruel to each other. I knew that I would have to try to protect Ronny from the barrage of teasing that could potentially come his way. I also knew that I could only do so much. That is because Ronny only had one arm.

More than 200 eighth graders had just spent two days in the woods learning about everything from tying knots to wildflower identification to outdoor cooking and more. On the third day, students had to apply their knowledge and newly developed skills in an Olympic-themed competition that had a reputation for being fierce. I tried to tell my students that it was not all about winning, but that teamwork and cooperation were vital to making the day successful. My motivational words hit the floor with a thud as these kids desired to do nothing less than bring home the gold.

Students worked together to come up with a solid plan for the challenging tire traverse, the hardest part of the day-long competition. Out of the 21 students in the class, only 18 could participate in this particular event. I told them that three people would have to voluntarily step out, or I would draw names randomly. I reminded them that everything would be done in a fair and diplomatic way. However, the elephant in the room was ready to stomp loudly on the ground and make itself known.

Two girls immediately volunteered to step out, but I had to draw a name out of a hat for the third person. I saw many eyes glance at Ronny, hoping he would raise his hand and join the girls. He did not. I felt the class teetering on the brink of anarchy and held my breath in fear of someone suggesting that Ronny sit out because of his handicap. No one said a word but the tension in the room was palpable.

I drew out a name, and, as chance would have it, I saw "Jay" on the slip of paper. He was the notorious ringleader of the class, athletic and competitive, with great leadership skills to boot. I could sense the disappointment in the room, but thankfully no one voiced a concern. Jay came up to me later and said, "Mrs. Eich, Ronny cannot cross the tires. He should be the one sitting out, not me." I sternly told Jay that I would rather lose every portion of the competition than hurt anyone's feelings. It was not all about winning, but I could see by the look on Jay's face that he didn't agree with me. He walked away, sorely disappointed.

As the competition drew near, Ronny approached me. "Mrs. Eich," he said, "I have decided not to do the tire traverse. I want Jay to go in my place." I asked him if this was truly his decision. I wondered if some members of the class had coerced him into backing out, but he assured me that it was his choice. Ronny's expression didn't give anything away, so I accepted his decision to withdraw from the event. I also spoke to Jay, who promised me that he had said nothing to Ronny. In my heart I hoped he was telling me the truth.

The greatly anticipated Olympic day finally arrived. The point of the competition was to work collaboratively as a team with unity, cooperation and a positive attitude. I marveled at the way students used their many talents and skills to answer tough questions and solve difficult problems. They were doing a great job but one event still loomed ahead.

The class finally approached the fateful tire traverse station. During this event students helped each other across the tires while making challenging maneuvers, crossing from one tire to the next. The most difficult part of the event occurred when two students had to crisscross in midair on a single tire without plummeting to the ground. If anyone fell, he or she had to start over, which took precious time off the clock. After several nerve-wracking moments, our team finished with time to spare and felt good about their accomplishments. I breathed a sigh of relief as I knew that this event could have divided the classmates and hurt the feelings of a special boy.

The lady in charge of the station told my class that since everyone had finished early, they had some free time. Jay piped up, "Mrs. Patton, could we go again with Ronny this time?"

She looked at him and said, "Sure, why not?"

The next five minutes would be forever etched in my mind as the highlight of my teaching career. I watched as 20 eighth graders took their classmate, Ronny, through the tire traverse with ease. Some spotted below while others helped him carefully cross from one side of a platform to the other. At times, they almost had to lift him from one tire to the next, but they did it together. I will never forget the huge grin beaming across Ronny's face as his classmates cheered him on, chanting in unison, "Ronny, Ronny!" He finally made it to the other side where he lifted a fist high in the air, proclaiming, "I did it!" There was not a dry eye among the parents and teachers who witnessed this heartwarming adolescent miracle. Every time I thought of that moment, even several years later, I would choke up again.

My class did not win the tire traverse event, but at the end of the award ceremony there was one special trophy left to present. The emcee announced that my class had won the coveted Spirit Award. Because of their teamwork and the positive way they encouraged and supported each other, they had earned the most prestigious award of all. When Jay nudged Ronny to go up and receive the award on behalf of our class, I could not have been more proud of either young man. Our entire class then ran up to and surrounded Ronny, who held the trophy high in the air. That image is forever engraved in my heart, and I am thankful to have worked with such a terrific bunch of young people. They inspired me.

Students are supposed to learn from their teacher, but my kids taught me a valuable lesson that day. Good things can come out of the most challenging circumstances if we let them. When I look back at that pinnacle moment, what could have been a tragedy instead turned into a moment of triumph.

I still smile and think of Ronny from time to time and wonder whatever happened to him. I have no doubt that he, too, remembers the day that he accomplished something miraculous with the help of his middle school friends.

Becoming a Kid Hero

The perfect way to start a family

Kathy McAfee

W E TOLD THEM not to call. We didn't want to know, either way. It was Christmas Eve and we wanted a little peace; a break from the emotional, financial and physical rollercoaster of the IVF process. But they didn't listen to our request. They called anyway.

"Hello. This is Betty from Dr. Zouves' office. I know you instructed us not to call, but the doctor thought you might want to hear this. [Pause] You're pregnant," she said.

That perhaps was the most glorious Christmas Eve that I can remember. We cried, we hugged, we yelled out loud. Finally we got a break after three years of trying to start a family. The embryo had taken hold and we were on our way.

It was great to experience the physical and emotional changes of pregnancy: the swollen breasts; the insatiable urge to eat turkey jerky; the joy of telling everyone that we knew about our good news; the feeling of victory and extreme gratitude and blessing.

The bubble burst 10 weeks later as we went for our second ultrasound. From the look on the technician's face, we knew in an instant that something was terribly wrong. Trained well in what not to say, she stated calmly, "Let me get the doctor." Our "little peanut" as we had come to call the life inside of me, had ceased. "Failure to thrive" is what I remember the medical explanation to be. It was hard to take it all in. It was even harder to tell the family and friends with whom we had shared the news, perhaps prematurely.

In the spirit of continued body invasion, they ordered a D&C to ensure that all of the tissue was removed from my body. They told me that I could try again in two or three months. The good news was that I could get pregnant, they said. I had a hard time finding the good in that.

The next few months went by like a blur. Amazingly, a good friend in a different state volunteered to be a surrogate parent for us, having our embryo implanted her body. She was willing to carry it to term and then sign over her "parental rights" to us upon the baby's birth. It all sounded pretty complicated and after speaking to an attorney who specialized in such matters, we realized that this route was not for us.

I remember thinking about the injustice of it all. It seems that teen girls could get pregnant just by thinking about sex. Some women who were not emotionally or financially capable of caring for children were popping them out like rabbits. I thought about the years that I had been on birth control, all the while my "plumbing" was blocked, unbeknownst to me. I grew angry at the country doctor who told me that I wasn't getting pregnant because I was "too stressed" or "too thin." His best medical advice was to drink wine and relax; or gain some weight. Albeit well meaning, this incompetent doctor squandered two years of my fertile life. Yes, I was well into the anger stage of the grieving process.

Little did we know that our thin thread moment was close at hand.

It happened in a movie theater. We arrived early to enjoy the trailers. We purchased an overpriced, over-salted bucket of popcorn and settled in to the red velour seats to escape at the movies. Before the official theatrical trailers were to start, they showed local advertising. As a marketing professional, I was aghast at the poor quality graphics and bad copy of these local ads. Why on earth anyone would advertise at the theater? Did they really think they would get any return on this off-beat advertising investment?

There were ads for the local car dealership; the local jewelry store; the restaurant where you could get a free appetizer if you brought your movie ticket in after the show. There were a few public service announcements, including one for foster care. The headline mentioned something corny like, *Be a Kid Hero*. It was all very innocuous.

Then the ads rotated through again. The *Be a Kid Hero* ad for foster care/adoption cycled through once more. Without saying a word, Byron and I turned and glanced at each other. It was a show stopper. We had our answer. This was our destiny.

Fast forward 10 years. We are the proud adoptive parents of Wilberto and Alberto—the "Ferrari twins," as my friend likes to call them. They came to live with us as foster children when they were seven-and-a-half years old. We "dated" for a while, lived together for more than a year and then chose to become an adoptive family. Despite their challenging start to life (removed from their bio family at age two due to a combination of neglect, substance abuse and domestic violence), they have adjusted well to their new family, new community and new life.

When I reflect back upon our challenges with infertility, I am happy to say that the blessings have definitely outweighed the pain and losses. Certainly, the passing of time has helped, as has having an instant family. Now that the twins are entering their teen years, Byron and I often find ourselves saying to each other, "What were we thinking?" or "This was your idea" or "We want our life back." These are typical parenting emotions, I imagine. They say that raising a family is one of the most challenging jobs you can ever have.

But seriously, I am grateful for the opportunity to have learned about my body, to have closely observed the advances in medical science and to have experienced the miracle of life first hand. Most of all, however, I am inspired by the lessons that I gained through this personal experience. So, if I may, let me now share with you what I learned:

- You can't control everything in your life.
- If you can't be reproductive, be productive.
- If you can't create a life, then save a life.
- Movie theater advertising works!

For more information on how you can become a kid hero and add to or create your own family through foster care and adoption, check out these web sites:

- http://www.heartgalleryofamerica.org/
- http://www.adoptuskids.org/
- http://www.caseyfamilyservices.org/

College Isn't For Girls

Breaking the rules

Nancy Julien Kopp

I MADE A CAREER decision by the time I finished second grade. I wanted to be a teacher. At home, I voiced my intention many times, but my mother never responded with enthusiasm. More often than not, she ignored the statements I made about being a teacher, but it didn't deter me one bit. I envisioned myself standing before a classroom, imparting knowledge, so my mother's indifference failed to upset me.

In 1953, I signed up for the college preparatory course when registering for high school. My parents didn't understand. Neither one had finished high school nor knew anything about college. And being a teen, I never bothered to discuss it with them at length.

Dad attended high school for three months before his father died suddenly. Those were the Depression years, so he had no choice but to leave school and work to support his mother and himself. Mom was more educated because she finished a full year of high school, but then quit to help her mother in a small family bakery. Their educations had ended.

Early in my senior year, I mentioned college more often, but I found no encouragement at home. Mom's mouth set firmly whenever I spoke of continuing my education, but I never wavered on my intent to teach. I would not let her deflate my dream.

One day after school, I helped Mom put groceries away. "Miss Horner, my dean, called me into her office today," I said. "She thinks I'd prefer Illinois State Normal University instead of Blackburn." I picked up two cereal boxes.

Mom grabbed hold of me as I turned to put the cereal in the pantry. "Now listen to me," she said. Her voice matched the fury in her eyes and the firm grip on my arm. "You have got to get this college idea out of your head. College isn't for girls. We have three boys to educate. They need good jobs. You don't!"

If she'd struck me with a doubled-up fist, I couldn't have felt any worse. Not go to college? After I'd lived with the dream for years? Tears welled in my eyes and slipped unchecked down my cheeks. I ran to the bathroom where I could cry alone. Seeds of resentment toward my mother were sowed that day.

That night after a quieter-than-usual dinner, Dad said that we had better talk about the crazy idea I had about going to college. "No one in our entire family has ever gone to college," he said. "What makes you think you're worthy of going? What makes you think we have that kind of money?" He took a long swallow of his coffee, and an edge of steel coated his voice when he went on. "Your mother's right. You have three younger brothers and if anyone is going to college, it will be them."

It meant the end of the conversation. I had no chance to

explain my case. In the mid-1950s among working-class families, higher education existed for boys and a few fortunate
girls, but obviously not for me. The lucky girls who continued
to study after high school became teachers or nurses. Others
went to work in an office, a factory or the retail world, clerk-
ing for a pittance until they married. My anger and resentment
flared, but I didn't voice it. In my family, only the adults won
arguments.

The next day, I woke up as determined to go to college as
I'd been the morning before. I could not, would not, accept
my parents' declaration. Somehow, I'd pack my suitcase in the
fall and go to college. I continued to consult with the dean at
the high school, never telling her what happened at home.

Mom continued her mantra of "college isn't for girls." One
day, she even said she felt bad about it, but the boys had to
come first. They would be the head of the household as adults,
and I probably wouldn't. We were all spaced several years
apart, and I knew she probably pictured a long period where
the three boys needed financial help to finish their education.

When the time came to fill out the college application, I
confessed to the dean, forced to tell her I'd failed at home. I
spoke haltingly, head down, my voice almost too soft for her
to hear. She questioned me at length, determining that money
proved to be part of the problem and that gender was another
difficulty. "Let's not call this the end," she said as I rose to
leave. I left her office daring to hope again.

A few days later, after we'd finished dinner, I began to clear
the table while my parents drank their coffee. "Sit down," Dad
said. He acted nervous, stuttered a little as he began, but then

his voice grew firm. "If you want to go to college, we'll find a way. I never had the chance, so maybe you should."

My heart did a flip-flop until I saw Mom's expression. My brothers and I left the kitchen when Dad gestured to us. I listened as raised voices and heated words enveloped our tiny kitchen and swirled through the rest of our apartment. I sat on the sofa trembling a little, hands clasped in prayer, while the boys played a game.

Finally, Dad came into the living room, face flushed, hands in his pockets. "Send the application in." He'd had the final word, and from that moment on, he became the supportive parent. My mother never did agree, but she didn't argue any longer either.

What had moved Dad to change his mind? I never knew, but I wondered if Miss Horner had contacted him. The '50s was an era when many children were not given explanations, and to my parents, I was still a child. Perhaps they'd agreed to keep it secret. If so, Dad never revealed it.

Soon after the decision, Miss Horner helped me fill out an application for a scholarship offered by the Panhellenic Society, and she put me on a list to receive a state scholarship as well. My dream and reality grew closer when I received each award.

Four years later, my parents attended my graduation on a hot June day. The gratefulness in my heart surely matched the pride in their eyes as I accepted my degree. The resentment I'd harbored all those years disappeared as well.

I became the first person in my extended family to attend college, followed by all three of my brothers. The four of us

worked and contributed to our education, we earned schol-
arships, and my parents sacrificed in ways that we probably
never knew. In our family, the desire to attend college finally
took precedence over all other considerations.

I don't believe I fully appreciated what my father had done
for me until it was too late to tell him, too late to thank him.
My own parenting years brought the entire episode into focus,
and I realized the great gift my dad had given with love.

A Man Named Beecher Goodin

The gift of an airport delay

Cathy Brown

I MET BEECHER GOODIN in Chicago's O'Hare Airport one stormy evening in April, 2006.

He changed my life.

I'd been attending a ladies' conference and was on my way to meet my family in Florida. A violent storm had shut down O'Hare, and the terminal was full of stranded passengers who were irritated and frustrated. I was stuck, too, disappointed that my family was beginning vacation without me. And I was still reeling from a very "trying" five-and-a-half months.

To make a long, painful story short, thanks to a slow responding insurance company, a dishwasher leak in our home had turned into a total kitchen remodel. We'd been forced to live without a working kitchen for more than five months!

Only once during that entire time did anyone invite us to dinner. My brother lives only 30 minutes away, yet we ate Thanksgiving dinner in a restaurant! Another family at church had experienced something similar, and I'd seen people rally around them, offering all sorts of help. I was so hurt and confused by the total lack of compassion we'd experienced.

Before you think I'm selfish, please understand—I used

to not want help from anybody. I'd survived struggles with infertility, my ex-husband's infidelity and drug abuse, years of single parenthood, a brother-in-law's suicide—God saw me through it all, humbling me, teaching me that I needed to accept help from people.

So what happens when the help is not offered?

I'd struggled, wondered, re-evaluated things, and prayed... and then, on that stormy night in the Chicago airport, I saw God.

In the waiting area for several flights, a sweet old man sat in a wheelchair, smiling peacefully as he watched some children scampering playfully around him.

I struck up a conversation with this man – there was a peace about him that drew me in. It started as casual, rather mindless chit chat. But there was nothing mindless about him. His name was Beecher Goodin and he announced his name with a pride that told me he was a child of God, and knew it.

The man started telling me stories – he was such a great storyteller – stories of his wife, children and parents. And as each story came alive, his eyes danced and twinkled, and it became clear that God was using this man's life stories to teach me and to comfort me. I heard his stories filled with such love, life and family, that it helped me to refocus on how greatly I have been blessed, and how the recent disappointments were only temporary and almost meaningless in the big picture.

As the hours crept by, I listened and learned from this wise old man. I suggested that he write his stories down. His face lit up and, with those dancing eyes, he told me proudly that he was writing a book – with his children's help! He was so proud and happy. He promised me a copy and I gave him my address, secretly thinking that it'd most likely get lost as he scribbled it into a tattered little notebook. Another one of those promises people make, I thought; full intentions to honor it, but life eventually takes over and the promise slips away, unacknowledged.

Soon we noticed that people were slowly disappearing from the gate area as, one by one, flights went from being delayed to cancelled. The airport – once bustling and chaotic – was becoming quieter, almost ominous, as the weather outside raged. It was as if God had created this special time just for me, and commanded the weather to cooperate so I could spend more time in the presence of Beecher Goodin!

Hunger pangs reminded me I hadn't eaten, and suddenly I realized that neither had Beecher Goodin. He didn't seem the least bit concerned about the bedlam going on all around him – cell phones, fast food, crying babies, frazzled travelers – Beecher Goodin was a peaceful oasis in the middle of chaos. And the circle of peace was broadening to touch those around him.

I bought some food for both of us. He was so grateful – and I suddenly realized he was alone. No one to help him. No one to check on his flight. No one to help him out of his chair to use the bathroom. Like almost every other traveler that night, I'd called someone to make alternative plans, or to reassure them I was OK. But Beecher Goodin hadn't! When I asked if there was someone he should call, he said his daughter was waiting for him but he didn't have a phone. I was so ashamed that I hadn't asked him sooner. I asked him for his daughter's number so I could call her and reassure her that her wonderful father was just fine; he fumbled about and again produced his little notebook. As he rummaged through the worn, tattered pad of paper, I saw page after page of handwritten notes and numbers, as if this tiny notebook contained a sort of precious documentation of his life. It took both of us to find his daughter's number.

I called and left as thorough a message as I could, but my flight was different from Beecher Goodin's. I had no idea what was going to happen to him, or when or if he'd get on another plane, or where he'd spend the night.

As it turns out, the family whose children were playing nearby was on the same flight as Beecher Goodin. The man graciously agreed to help him to the restroom. And as the airport terminal completely emptied, the once noisy, bustling gates were now eerily empty and silent. The restaurants and food stands had closed for the night, leaving no prospect for food. It seemed as if there were only a few of us left in the entire airport – me, this sweet, Godly man, and the young family I'd have to entrust him to.

And I trusted them. They'd played a role in teaching me what I'd so ignorantly wondered about earlier – what happens when the help doesn't come? How could I have been so sad and selfish, wondering why people hadn't helped me and my family during what I'd thought were tough times?

I'd known all along exactly what happens when help doesn't come. You go help someone else.

The eyes truly are the window into a person's soul. Beecher Goodin smiled as he hugged me goodbye that evening in

April, 2006, and his eyes twinkled. I saw his soul. And it was beautiful.

*****

Those few hours with Beecher Goodin were a precious gift and an integral part of my spiritual journey; I was born again not long after my encounter with Beecher Goodin. I praise God that He had placed me in that airport, at that gate, at that time, in that chair, next to that man.

My family has since moved out of the house with the brand new kitchen. A few days ago, I received a package at our new address. A book arrived from Beecher Goodin. He'd remembered! And so had I. God is so good.

In Health and in Sickness

Witnessing the depth of true love

Virginia Cassarino-Brown

I T WAS THE gentle grasp of her rigid fingers, the knowing look in his eyes that caught my attention. He led her
down the smooth wooden stairs of Split Rock. Cool dewy
grass stretched out before them waiting to kiss their feet.
The warm, morning sun sprinkled patterns of light on their
rounded shoulders. Her slow, deliberate steps made the rela-
tively short distance from camp to lake seem daunting.

My level of discomfort was palpable, but I could not take
my eyes off them. For a second I thought, "Is this how a voyeur
feels?" I knew I was intruding on an intimate moment, but I
was mesmerized by their unwavering determination. Finally,
they reached the shoreline, and he guided her into the crisp
water for her early morning swim.

For 15 summers, I have witnessed Billie commune with the
lake. As a neighbor, I had a front row seat from the comfort
of my porch swing. While drinking a warm cup of coffee, I
wondered if the water was too cold or too rough, if the air too
chilly or too windy. Billie, on the other hand, could swim for
endless periods of time. She would find sweet surrender swimming in the cool, clear waters of Mooselookmeguntic Lake. I

marveled at her ability to seemingly sprout fins and gills. In my mind's eye, she breathed life into the lake.

Billie and Henry are more than 30 years older than my husband and I, but somehow age is not relevant in determining who becomes your friends. I could not ask for better camp neighbors. Actually, we progressed from acquaintances to steadfast friends quite effortlessly.

Their camp is right next to ours. The buildings sit side by side, barely 50 feet apart. Each property has its own weathered west-facing dock decorated with a hodgepodge of outdoor furniture that invites you to indulge in a summer cocktail. More often than not, we found ourselves together, enjoying each other's company, drinks in hand, spending the five o'clock hour discussing the day. While soaking in the sunset, our conversations would cover a myriad of topics: the weather, the moose spotted in town, the fiddler's contest in the village, Billie's anticipated coleslaw for our Fourth of July celebration, etc.

Nine months out of each year we do not reside next to one another. Billie and Henry live in Maryland, and we live on the coast of Maine, but somehow, the separation does not weaken our friendship. We seem to be able to pick up where we left off the previous Labor Day when we said our farewells. But now life is different.

Six months ago, Billie was diagnosed with Amyotrophic Lateral Sclerosis (ALS). The cruel, harsh debilitation of this progressive, neurodegenerative disease has slowly, doggedly decreased her ability to begin her daily ritual independently. She is no longer able to walk to the water unattended. She sometimes forgets places and names. Her smile still brightens her face, but her eyes tell a different story.

Yet, as I watch them from the safety of my world, I notice that Henry is ever there for her with gentle words, a guiding hand, a reassuring look. He says to me matter-of-factly, "It's the cards we've been dealt." I wonder, is this pretense for my benefit?

I ponder what it must be like to share a lifetime with someone, raise children together, share successes, failures, triumphs and heartaches. What is it like to know someone so intimately, yet have to watch her succumb to an unforgiving disease that will ultimately rob her of a graceful passing? Is it a burden? It must be. How can it not be?

Then all of a sudden, it became clear to me. I think back to 27 years ago when I shared marriage vows with my husband. We spoke familiar words, common place phrases one hears at every wedding. At the time, we didn't give them much thought, yet those simple words have a powerful significance. This is what loving, cherishing and honoring someone in sickness means. It is now, while watching Henry guide Billie by his gentle touch on the small of her back, that I see two people carrying out their promise to each other. There is no burden here. There is only a bond that knows no distance between them. It is that same bond of love and compassion that I feel with my husband, and I know without a doubt that he will be there for me, and I will be there for him, to honor all the significance of our marriage vows.

The discomfort and uneasiness I felt while watching Billie and Henry from my porch swing is no longer there. I smile from a distance as they lean on each other. Their devotion to one another comforts me. I am bearing witness to something beautiful. When Henry looks at Billie or talks about her, his face smiles. The crinkles around his eyes deepen. His lopsided grin widens. He radiates such love and affection. It's as if he is truly unburdened, happy for another day. He doesn't measure time by noticing how weak she is or by what she can no longer do. He measures it by reveling in another day with his Billie.

It's that simple, that poignant. How full and rich their lives still are—for however long, in health and in sickness.

My Father's Gift: Dementia

The turnaround that sustained me

Lucy Parker Watkins

T HE MIND IS a miraculous collection of highly orga-
nized tangles of associations that philosopher John
Locke believed begins as a clean slate, or *tabula rasa*, only to
be developed through life experiences and cognitive development. Could the reverse of this be true? Is it possible those
who develop dementia experience an unraveling of their
wiring that ultimately releases the mind so it might redirect
an adult toward pure essence? And, if so, do these people end
as they began, as tabulae rasae?

It was in May of 2008 that doctors discovered my father
had suffered a series of previously undiagnosed mini-strokes,
as well as three forms of dementia. As a result, he needed constant care. Understandably, I feared a decision to assist in his
care would threaten the little healing I'd managed during our
most recent estrangement. Since my father and I always had
a highly dysfunctional and extremely painful relationship
involving abuse, severe alcoholism, and a whole slew of negative behaviors, this was the relationship I worked to overcome.
In short, my life as his youngest child was a test in survival.
He was my only living parent and I had focused much of my

energies trying to help him see my value as his daughter. It took me more than 30 years to realize I was wasting my time.

Ultimately, I realized two reasons to help my father. Firstly, my sister shouldn't have to do it on her own. Secondly, it was probably the last chance I would have to find closure in a relationship that might otherwise haunt me the rest of my life. As I told him during one his lucid moments, when he expressed surprise that I was visiting him, "I need closure in our relationship and since you have never made a recognizable move, I realize I must be present to allow the opportunity for this part of my healing to occur. I can either be the daughter who dances on your grave or I can be the one who weeps when you die." This seemed to make an impression, but his anger and bitterness, alcoholism and depression continued to be the crux of his identity.

In the beginning, there was some improvement in his dementia symptoms, but that was temporary and unpredictable. He spent most of his time not knowing anything of the outside world and very little of his immediate environment, even though he was in a home he had known since 1955. One day he would greet me with a smile. Another day he would stand in front of me telling me to "put up your dukes and fight me." Generally, he didn't know who I was. Anger, rage, foul language, tears and emotional venom remained the most obvious components of our relationship.

Admittedly, I found relief in the fact that he usually didn't know me during my semi-weekly visits. I hid behind the veil of his dementia for my own sense of sanity. During this time, I took advantage of those days he had no idea who I was. Each time I walked into his house, carrying groceries and clean laundry, I acted as a paid employee. Each time, he bared his teeth at me with an audible growl of hatred.

Time and time again, well-meaning experts tried to explain his behavior as symptoms of dementia, but I knew that wasn't the case. My father was continuing to exist as he had since 1972. Contrary to traditional medical beliefs, his dementia seemed to manifest in occasional bouts of kind, gentle behavior, the opposite of textbook accounts of the effects of dementia.

Then, after nearly a year of what can only be described as my father exhibiting sheer hatred towards me, he looked at me and asked, "Why is it I don't know who you are but I know I absolutely hate you?"

"Because you do," I said. "Since I can remember you have been an angry, hateful man. When mom got sick, you got sick too. You drank too much. You tried to kill yourself. I was the one who poured out urine from a bottle because you were too drunk to get up and do it yourself. I was the one to find you bloody from another suicide attempt. I was the victim of your demise. Having me help you now must feel a bit like Hitler would have felt had Jews been in charge of finding care for him had he survived the war. I am the one person who knows the truth."

I expected my father to react in his usual fashion, but this time he did not yell at me for my honesty. For the first time in my life, my father did not make excuses for his behavior. He responded rather than reacted and asked, "I did all that? I treated you that way?"

"Yes, Dad. And there's much more to the story."

"I am so sorry," he said. "I am sorry I put you through all of that. I am sorry I failed as your father. You didn't deserve any of it."

I had been hoping for this moment since I was seven years old. I had worked tirelessly to overcome him, our relationship, the abuse and the pain. There were successes along the way, but this seemingly sincere apology touched me so deeply, so profoundly, that I felt years of burden, heartache and my deep sense of inadequacy slowly peel away, one hardened layer at a time, over the course of the next few weeks.

There was also an undeniable change in his usual reactions. He became, for lack of a better term, simple. It was as if the dementia removed memories and emotional habits, nearly stripping him of his usual hostility towards me.

This chain of events has fueled my belief that as his mind has failed he has begun the last leg of a round-trip journey to his original essence, to tabula rasa. I no longer identify him as a man who is nearly incapable of feeling empathy or understanding his effect on the emotional environment in our family. The memory loss has somehow cleared his slate and refreshed his psyche. For if he still had these defenses, if he still had the complete memories of all the experiences he deems as injustices, he would continue to be incapable of seeing my truth and his role in it. He would certainly have remained incapable of making such an apology.

In this way, dementia has been a gift to our relationship. It has cleansed him. It has helped to further cleanse me. And while we still have obstacles in his care, he is, for the first time

in my life, a father to me: a father who is happy to see me; a
father who imparts bits of wisdom that have been unearthed
by the release of memories, anger and bitterness; a father who
seems to genuinely love me. I am no longer the daughter who
will dance on his grave when he dies. I will most certainly be
the daughter who weeps.

An Unlikely Guardian Angel

The freedom of prayer

Sheila Appleby Williams

I N 1994, I was a single mother working full time as a special education teacher at a small elementary school located in a quiet residential neighborhood in Los Angeles. My days were stressful from the moment the first bell rang shrilly at 8 a.m.

However, I didn't learn the real meaning of stress until my strong-willed and challenging daughter turned 14 and her raging hormones and teenage rebellion swept over my world like a tornado. Sex, drugs and running away were on her agenda and the threat of my ex-husband's vengeful, "I'm letting her do whatever she wants; she's never coming back to you," replayed razor sharp through my mind all the day.

These were not the sort of problems to be discussed in the teacher's lounge; even close friends could offer no assistance and little comfort.

Mr. Bryant was the night custodian at the school. His six-foot, 300-pound linebacker body filled the doorway and would have been quite intimidating were it not for his gentle demeanor and kindly boyish bespectacled face.

At the end of the school day, I usually sat at my desk with my shoulders hunched over and my face turned down on top of piles of student papers waiting to be graded. I was trying to summon the strength to make the 45-minute drive home on the crowded freeways.

Mr. Bryant's shift was just beginning and he would routinely start in my classroom, sweeping, emptying trash cans and making polite chit-chat. One day, with a warm smile, he asked, "How ya doin', Ms. Williams? Tough day?" By doing so, he triggered the anxiety and worst scenarios buried in my brain and I began telling him of my agonizing concerns about my daughter's welfare. He stopped his work, leaned on his broom and listened intently to my recitation of her delinquent and dangerous behaviors.

Mr. Bryant was no stranger to the dark side of life. He had grown up in South Central Los Angeles and had seen many friends and family members get involved in gangs and drugs, drop out of school and virtually ruin their lives.

Mr. Bryant shared his thoughts about the situation and disclosed that he was studying to be a minister. I was somewhat surprised but he was a private person and usually focused on being a good listener rather than talking about himself. He said that he would pray for my daughter and have his congregation pray for her as well. Just being able to unburden myself in talking to him and feeling confident that I could trust him and his warmth and sincere caring gave me some much-needed comfort that day.

A short time after that conversation, I transferred to another school closer to my home and lost touch with Mr. Bryant.

Since that time 14 years have passed. My daughter, through

a somewhat miraculous series of events, got back on track, got her GED at a continuation school, held down a full-time job and ultimately went back to school and graduated from UCLA.

She started a successful career as a commercial realtor and is living a healthy and productive life. We enjoy a close relationship and rarely talk about those days.

Recently, I was visiting a friend I hadn't seen in a long time who had been a teacher at that same elementary school. She said, "I almost forgot to tell you. I went by the school last week and saw Mr. Bryant, the custodian. He remembered that we were friends and asked how you were doing. He said that after you left the school, he was cleaning out your room and found a picture you had left in your desk of you and your daughter. He put it in his Bible and says he has prayed for you and her every day for the last 14 years. Isn't that amazing?"

It was amazing and I was so touched by this man's spiritual "gift" to us for all these years.

A few days later I called Mr. Bryant. He didn't sound at all surprised to hear from me and said that he had just looked at our picture that morning and said his prayers for us.

As it turns out, we were not the only beneficiaries of Mr. Bryant's prayers. There are several teachers with health problems whom he prays for; the adopted children of a relative; an elderly aunt. Mr. Bryant made the time to pray for all the people in need who had the good fortune to cross his path. I assumed he was a minister by now, but no, as it turned out, "there were too many restrictions, and I need to have the freedom to help people in my way."

I have never been a traditionally religious person, but I do sincerely believe that Mr. Bryant has been my daughter's guardian angel during those desperately difficult times and continues to be a blessing to all who know him.

The Maw-Maw Sweater

The greatest graduation gift

Joyce E. Sudbeck

WHY IN THE world would anyone want to start college at the ripe age of 43? I suppose I did look a little out of place in a lecture hall full of kids who were barely in their 20s. Nonetheless, the snide smiles and curious looks of my classmates didn't faze me a bit. I was there for a purpose, and what they thought really didn't matter.

My study habits were better and my personal achievement expectations higher than most of my classmates. Maturity paid off, big time, in this arena. I sat in the front row of every class so as not to be distracted by the "not-so-interested" students. I religiously completed all my homework and assignments. I studied hard for every exam. When the grades were posted, my name was at the top of the "A" list. Hard work paid off.

The incentive for furthering my education was to earn a promotion I felt I deserved. I had a good job, albeit a nontechnical one, with pay far below technician's level. In the lab, I worked side by side with the technicians. Since we were short-staffed, my job responsibilities had grown into the technical area, and I was performing the same duties as the technicians were, just not being paid for it.

Although I was already doing the work, company policy would not permit me to be promoted without the formal education that I didn't have. The minimum requirement for a technician position was four semesters of college level science, with two labs. Human Resources advised that the job duties I had performed during the past two years would equal one semester of science. Without fulfilling the remaining educational requirements, however, I would never receive the promotion.

Thus, I paid my tuition, put my books in a tote bag and off I went to college.

Once I provided documentation of completing three semesters of college-level science, I was immediately promoted to technician.

By that time, I had become accustomed to the class routine and found that I enjoyed learning after all these years. My husband and I talked about the advantage of continuing college and even pursuing a degree. It would make my current skills more marketable and possibly open more opportunities for me in the future. I decided to stay in college. It was in my fifth year of college that our first grandchild, Emily, was born. Eighteen months later her little sister came along. Then our daughter had her first—a boy—a month after that.

It was hard to remain focused on studies with these new interests in my life. I did manage to balance it all, still forging ahead toward my goal, while working full time. At times it was difficult, but obviously not impossible.

The Christmas before my long-awaited June graduation, I gave Emily a little sweater I had knitted in my practically non-existent spare time. I had spotted a pattern for a long-sleeved sweater in her size and knew it was something I just had to make for her. It was so much fun. A real labor of love. I struggled to squeeze in knitting time in order to get it finished before Christmas, and I did.

It was very soft yarn, lilac colored, with white edging all the way around. I put a small, appliquéd white dove on the left chest side with tiny white buttons down the front. Around the neck I had sewn a row of white lace. Emily looked darling in it, and it fit perfectly.

Emily didn't take it off all Christmas evening. Her mother told me that from that day forward, she put it on every day, wearing it every time they left the house. People would comment on what a pretty sweater she was wearing, and she would say, "Maw-Maw Sweater." Emily would not take the sweater off long enough for her mother to wash it. She would have to grab the sweater, at night, after Emily was in bed to rinse it out. Obviously, the sweater had been a big hit with my granddaughter.

The months flew by, and graduation night rolled around. I was so excited. I had kept my nose buried in my books for seven years, and now I would be free to relax and free from pressure. Especially since the grandchildren had come along, I had been looking forward to the final semester of school coming to a close and to graduation.

Dressed in my robe and mortarboard, I anxiously awaited the ceremony. The children arrived, and we exchanged hugs and kisses.

Emily was wearing a blue and white pinafore and

underneath, a tee with white lace on the sleeves. She wore white Mary Janes and white socks with lace. Her hair was drawn up in two cow-tails secured by narrow blue and white ribbons. Since the evening was cool, her mom had laid out a new white sweater for her to wear. However, Emily had a different idea. Atop the crisp pinafore, she was wearing her "slightly soiled" lilac sweater, trimmed in white lace, with a dove on the left breast. Her "Maw-Maw Sweater." Her mother was full of apologies for the way Emily was dressed. She said she hoped I wasn't embarrassed. She had tried her best to get her to wear the new white sweater, but Emily was having none of it. Through crocodile tears she had protested, "No! No! Maw-Maw Sweater." Rather than continue fighting about the sweater and end up running late for the ceremony, her mother let her put on the lilac sweater. She brought the white sweater along, hoping to make the switch later. It didn't happen.

I looked down at my little granddaughter and a smile spread over my face. Could anyone be embarrassed by this beautiful child? Certainly, not me. I said, "She looks as sweet as she always does. Not to worry. She looks absolutely perfect."

The ceremony began. Those graduating "with honors" were called up first, to receive special recognition. I proudly received the gold braid to wear on my shoulder. We returned to our seats.

One by one, the graduates were called by name, up to the stage. Four alumni stood waiting to shake our hands and congratulate us on our achievement. The last alumnus gave each graduate a faux "diploma," rolled and tied with a ribbon.

Emily and her mother were waiting patiently with the camera, to snap my picture as I received my diploma. Emily was too short to see me while I was standing on the floor of the stage. Her mother took the picture, and I walked onto the top of the stairs where they stood below.

The minute Emily saw me, her face lit up and she exclaimed, excitedly, "Maw-Maw!" There she stood in her "slightly soiled" lilac sweater.

All the honors and acknowledgments I had received during that evening quickly faded in the face of that moment.

The greatest honor bestowed on me, by far, was the look of love for me on Emily's precious face and the unquestionable, distinguished honor of being called "Maw-Maw."

Seeing Eric

Believing in someone can change them

Ruth Lambert

O NE DAY I said "hello" to the man who delivered printed office forms to our small company. There was no answer—so I looked at him sharply. I was dismayed and horrified by what I saw. There before me stood a stereotypical picture out of the 1860s. A tall, slender black man in his middle 20s, he was a parody of "shiftlessness." His sneakers were torn and dirty, his shirt smelled of old sweat, and his tightly curled short hair was literally full of lint. He also shuffled as he walked, making a kind of harsh scuffing sound. When I said "hello" and looked at him, I saw that his head hung down, his shoulders were rounded, and his eyes were focused firmly on the floor.

I had recently read about the work of Martin Buber, trying to grasp his concept of "I and Thou." Buber seemed to be saying that by simply seeing others, really seeing them, as worthy human beings, we could transform daily experiences with rich moments of connection. I decided that I would connect with this man, no matter what, and that I would watch to see what happened.

I said "hello" again, and then asked his name. "Eric..." he

mumbled, still staring at the floor.

"THANK YOU, Eric," I said slowly and in a focused way, as I took the package from him. He shuffled off without a backwards glance.

That day, I issued an order to my staff: Whenever Eric arrived to drop off a print order, he was to be sent directly to my office. As the CEO and president of the company, I was often in meetings or on the phone when Eric arrived. Nonetheless, he was always sent in to see me. And I made sure to greet him personally when he arrived.

I always said, "Hello Eric. It is good to see you!" I watched as slowly, day by day, Eric's posture began to change. He entered my office confidently, and no longer stared at the floor. He looked back at me.

"Hello, M'am" he said one day, after a few weeks of my greetings.

"My name is Ruth," I countered. "I would be glad if you called me that." He glanced away again, clearly embarrassed.

"Yes, Miss Ruth," he mumbled. I decided that was fine, given his Deep South background, and the age difference between us.

"Thank you, Eric," I said again.

Over the next few months, I could see Eric visibly brighten and relax as he entered my office. His shoulders were held back, his neck and head high.

"Hello there, Miss Ruth," he'd say, often before I could greet him.

"Nasty weather out there, isn't it?" I'd venture on a stormy day.

"Sure is, M'am!" he would reply, laughing. We were now on friendly terms.

One day, I saw he had new, clean sneakers. "Eric, those are very nice sneakers. New?"

"Yes, Miss Ruth, they are." Eric beamed.

"Well," I said, "they look great."

A few days later, I noticed that Eric's tab collar shirt was clean, pressed and smelled sweet. "Wow," I said, "I see you've got a new shirt to go with those spiffy sneakers!" He grinned, showing fine white teeth. "Yes, M'am!" he fairly sang. "Ironed it myself."

Now, the changes came quickly. His hair, always lint-enhanced and uncombed, was suddenly clean, brushed and glowing with health. His hands were well groomed and clean. Each time he arrived, he looked more "put together" and self-aware.

"Tell me something about you," I said one day.

"Oh," he replied shyly, "I got a promotion at work. They told me I was doing my job better and they appreciated it."

"Wow," I said happily. "That's wonderful."

"It's my first raise, ever," he told me confidentially.

"Congratulations, Eric. I know you deserved it!" I was elated.

Our contact continued for several years in the same manner. Eric continued to progress in his life in remarkable ways. He took responsibility for his young daughter, and told me proudly when Carissa made the honor roll at her grammar school. During the 22 years I ran my small company, Eric continued to work for the printing company, finally managing a delivery crew of four drivers. He made sure that he always delivered our orders personally, always stopping in to see me in the executive office.

He drove his first new car into our parking lot and bounded up the steps to tell me, his voice full of excitement. He looked like a completely different man from the Eric I'd met six years earlier. He was still a tall, slim black man, but just about everything else was different. Self-confidence, natural friendliness and good humor shone from his eyes and radiated out toward everyone he met. He told me that his daughter was taking violin lessons, loved math and had applied to college. She would be the first family member to have that advantage. His love and pride lit up his face as he spoke.

At this stage of our relationship, Eric and I invariably gave each other a hug at the end of our encounters. I hugged him that day, and heaved a huge inward sigh of contentment and joy: Buber had been so right. Merely SEEING another human being can indeed have a profound effect. Where Eric gained a new life, I gained a new friend and a deeper appreciation of my fellow human beings.

Angie

Gifts can be found anywhere

I MET ANGIE IN December 1993, on a cold, cloudy day, on the train, on my dreaded trip to Beijing, after attending the funeral of my father in my hometown, the City of Lanzhou, some 1,200 miles west of the Chinese capital. My friend Kai had failed to secure me a plane ticket, and I had gotten on the train without a seat.

As the wind howled and darkness descended, the steam engine-powered train puffed and blew its way eastward, heaving, as it seemed to me, in inconsolable pain, much like my own sorrow. I started a trip to the city called "guilt" and loaded myself up with blame.

I dreaded and agonized over how I could pass the 34-hour journey as my mind was flooded with memories of my father. My father, the multi-talented poet and artist who walked his way from an impoverished village to the provincial capital and became the first university graduate in his home county. My father, who was persecuted many times because he had received a university education prior to the Communists' taking power and because he had married the daughter of a landowner. My father, who had single-handedly raised me after my mother perished during the Cultural Revolution. My father, the dedicated educator who poured his heart into nurturing the growth of his students whenever he was allowed during the lulls of political persecution imposed on him by the communist government. My father, who claimed to have had an elastic stomach that "shrank" so that his children could have bigger shares of meals when food was scarce. My father, who was proud to finally see his four children graduate from universities after the reforms made his background less of a liability in their careers. My father, who spent many sleepless nights following the situation in the Middle East, when I, his only daughter, covered the conflicts that stormed the Arabian deserts. My father, who, with much courage and understanding, accepted my decision to marry a white, English-speaking Canadian even though he did not speak English and could not communicate with my future husband.

I wondered how life would go on without my father. I regretted not having written to him after his last letter reaffirming his blessings to my pending union with Mike, my future husband, whom I had met in Kuwait during the Gulf War. I was angry with myself for not having called him on the first-ever telephone installed in his own apartment. I chided myself for not having had the courage to hug him when I saw him last, as public expressions of emotions between adults, including family members, were scorned upon at the time in China. Most of all, I felt guilty that I had not rushed home to his bedside when he became very ill and instead wasted precious time waiting for news from the Canadian Embassy on a visa that would eventually allow me to join Mike across the

Pacific.

A non-believer in supernatural powers, I found myself praying that somehow I could be given a chance to make up for my failure to give back to this extraordinary man who had nurtured me and hundreds of other people. I would do anything for such a chance to return the love I had received!

Soon after the train started, the loudspeaker broadcasted a shocking piece of news: A baby girl was found deserted on the train. The appeal went out to solicit help from doctors or nurses among the passengers.

Although neither a doctor nor a nurse, I felt I had to see the baby and offer help.

There she was! A beautiful baby girl with a round face, a thick head of black hair, dimples on her rosy cheeks and big sparkly eyes. A bundle of smiling joy, surrounded by a circle of strangers curious about what had happened to her.

A young woman, presumably the mother, had left the girl in the temporary care of a passenger for what was supposedly a short visit to the washroom. The woman never resurfaced. The baby was wrapped in a small cotton quilt, with half a bag of milk powder, a bottle, a few cotton diapers and 50 yuan (six dollars). No name. No address.

As most of the other passengers returned to their seats, I volunteered and was given the responsibility of caring for the baby for the rest of the journey, with the help of another passenger, a gentleman named Mr. Qi.

We decided to call the baby Yuan, or "sent by destiny." In English, Angie.

The stewardess arranged for a cabin in the sleeping car,

which Mr. Qi and I converted into a temporary haven for Angie and where I spent 32 of the most rewarding hours of my life.

I fed Angie when she was hungry. I cried when she cried, and I smiled with her when she smiled. I told her stories that my father had soothed me with when I fell sick in my early years. I recited to her poems with which my father had inspired my interest in literature as a student.

Mr. Qi, a man who had never had a chance to take care of his own children when they were young, took on the duties of washing diapers, which seemed to never dry fast enough before the baby was wet again. Mr. Qi, whose name meant "complete," decided to adopt Angie on behalf of his niece who had been trying to have a baby without success.

Angie seemed to be in a lot of pain, yet she responded to my stories and poems with the broad and carefree smiles of a true angel.

As minutes and hours passed, the burden of guilt with which I had boarded the train left me. In its place, a sense of joy and love enveloped me. The huff and puff of the steam engine became the symphony of comfort and affirmation of life.

Neither Mr. Qi nor I realized that the baby was born with a fatal disease, and Angie died a few days after we reached Beijing.

Brief as it was, my encounter with baby Angie taught me an important lesson: The best way to honor my father was to live life as he did—as an authentic, dignified, hard-working and caring human being. The meaning of life lies in giving.

The Hat

How a challenge changed the student and the teacher

Elynne Chaplik-Aleskow

IT STARTED AS a typical first class session of the new
semester at Wright College in Chicago. Twenty-five faces
were staring at me with the fear typical of college students
who would prefer to be anywhere in the world other than a
communication class. As I looked back at them with all the
empathy I could express, I asked that everyone wearing hats
please remove them. They looked at me with that confusion
of a generation unfamiliar with such etiquette.

The hats were removed except for one young man's. When
I asked him directly, he answered "no." I was shocked but did
not show it. Not 10 minutes into the session and in front of
new students, whom I was meeting for the first time, I was
being challenged. How I handled this moment could determine semester survival—my semester survival.

The students were intently watching me and waiting. It was
my move. I decided not to deal publicly with this challenge to
my authority so I asked to see the young man after class. His
name was Mark and he looked like the most unlikely of all the
students to express insubordination. He was slight in build,
clean cut with a pleasant face. He was not someone who stood

out from the others. Yet he had said "no" to a directive from his new Professor in front of new classmates on the first day of the new semester. There would be no choice. I had to convince him to do what the others were asked. He would have to back down.

After class, alone in my classroom, Mark and I faced one another. His eyes focused toward the floor. He would not look at me as I spoke. His hat, the symbol of his defiance, still sat securely on his head.

"Mark," I said softly, "you must follow the rules of this class. Removing your hat demonstrates respect. Is there a reason you feel you must wear your hat? I am willing to listen."

Mark lifted his eyes and looked into mine. "No," he answered. His look was empty. His tone was flat.

"Then you must remove it," I answered in my most professorial voice. He did as I asked.

At that moment I recognized my challenge with this young man. He complied in removing his hat but I had not reached him. I had forced him but I had not persuaded him.

Slowly throughout the semester, I felt a bond growing between Mark and me. Sometimes he would even smile at my jokes and ask thoughtful questions in class. When I saw him in the hall, he would tip his hat. I would not let him see me smile at that obvious gesture.

The final week of the semester Mark asked me to stay after class. He had something to tell me which he had kept secret.

I had come to know him as a gifted poet and hard working writer and speaker. He worked harder than most, perhaps, because Mark suffered from MS, which had affected his coordination and vocal cords. Some days the class and I understood him better than others.

"Do you remember the first day of class when I refused to remove my hat?" he asked.

"Oh yes I do," I answered.

"Well, now I would like to tell you why I did that. About a year ago I went to an open-mic forum to read my poetry. They laughed at me."

"They what?" I asked, not wanting to believe what I was hearing.

"They laughed."

His speech was labored and painfully slow. "I was humiliated."

Once again like that first day of class we were alone in my classroom. We looked at one another through our tears.

"The first day of this class when I refused to remove my hat I was trying to get you to throw me out of your class. The course was required but I did not want to ever stand before an audience again and perform my writing. But you would not give up on me. You would not let me leave."

"You chose to stay, Mark," I answered softly. We stood there for a moment, looking at one another.

For his final persuasive speech, Mark spoke on Stem Cell Research Funding. He passionately argued for our government to acknowledge that it is his quality of life they are ignoring and for his classmates to vote for legislators who would make the stem cell reality happen. Would it be soon enough for him we all agonizingly wondered?

After offering an articulate and informed argument, with

great difficulty Mark walked to his visual aid, which was an empty white poster board. He asked his audience to give him one thing. Only one thing. He picked up a marker and with a shaking hand one letter painstakingly at a time he wrote, "Hope."

A year after he had completed my course, Mark came to my office to say hello. He proudly told me that students from our class would stop him in the hall and tell him that they would never forget his last speech. The MS was progressive and he was suffering. Yet he looked happy and at peace. He had formed a team in his name for the MS Walk each year and was trying to raise money to help him and others through funding for research.

Three years later I received an e-mail from him. He wanted me to know that he was writing again and that for the first time since he had been traumatized by the experience he again performed his poetry in an open mic at a Chicago club. He said he could have never done it without my course and my friendship. In his last line he told me that he always wore his cherished hat.

Hospital Angel

A life-changing visit

Ferida Wolff

I T WAS AN early spring morning, the beginning of a day that
I would have loved to spend looking through gardening
catalogues and anticipating planting bulbs in my backyard.
Instead, I put on my jacket and headed for the hospital where
my mother was in the final stages of Alzheimer's disease. She
had laid in a semi-coma for several days now, her life force
decreasing day by day. Her doctor said that her physical sys-
tems were all shutting down at once. My sister, my father and
I held vigil from early morning until late at night, reluctant to
leave her.

That day I got to the hospital a little before them. I looked
in on Mom to see if anything had changed overnight. The
only change was more of the same: more wasting, more
labored breathing. The machine that monitored her heart
pinged softly next to her bed. The nurses assured me that she
was not in any pain, but I sure was. Watching the progress
of the disease was agonizing for me. I felt utterly helpless. I
couldn't make her well again and there was nothing I could do
to comfort her. She wasn't even aware that I was in the room.

My heart ached every time I saw my mother. Yet I hadn't

212

cried as I went through the distressing stages of the disease with her; not when she lost her ability to say ordinary words and started making up her own; or when her temperament turned harsh and she said things to my sister and me that we never heard from her before. I didn't cry when she couldn't remember where she lived or when common, everyday things confused her—a fork, a glass of water, a towel. I refused to cry when my mother forgot who I was. I knew she couldn't help it.

I stood at the end of her bed, listening to her heavy breathing. There was something I had to say to Mom but I was having trouble saying it. Finally, with my voice trembling, I spoke slowly, hoping that somehow, within that dense fog that surrounded her, she could hear me and understand what I was telling her. I told her that I loved her and thanked her for giving me the best she could. I said that my sister and I would help care for our father so that she didn't have to worry about him and that we would look after each other as well. Then I said the words that were the hardest thing I ever had to say: "You can leave in peace, Mom, whenever you are ready."

There was no response, not that I really expected one. I took a deep breath and went into the hallway to wait for my father and sister.

I was leaning against the wall when a woman came briskly around the corner. She started down the hall, then turned and came back to where I was standing.

"You look as if you could use a hug," she said.

I was about to say what I usually did when people asked how I was doing—that I was fine, thanks. But when I tried to speak, my throat closed and the words wouldn't come out. I suddenly felt more alone than I ever had in my life. The woman held out her arms. I fell into this stranger's embrace and finally wept, surprising myself with the intensity of my emotions. The woman didn't say a word. She just held me until the sobs stopped and I lifted my head.

"Thank you," was all I could manage to say.

She smiled and continued down the hall. I looked after her until my sister called to me and I turned around. When I got my voice back, I told her about the woman who had understood the pain I was feeling and so graciously offered her compassion.

"What woman?" my sister asked. She looked to where I pointed but there wasn't anyone there. The hallway was quiet and deserted.

"She must have gone into one of the other rooms," I said. My sister and father went into Mom's room and I went to the nurses' station to ask if anyone had seen which room the woman went into.

"We didn't see anyone," they said.

"She had come in just a short while ago," I insisted, "and walked that way."

They shrugged. I could see they were busy, perhaps too busy to take notice of someone moving briskly down the hall. I set off to look for her myself, to tell her how much I appreciated her kindness. I looked in all of the rooms but the woman wasn't in any of them. There was no way for her to have left without passing me, only she hadn't. Except for me and the busy nurses there had been no one in the hall.

Was she an angel? I wondered.

During the next days, I kept looking for the woman; I never saw her again. But in that brief encounter she left me with a new understanding of our role in other people's lives. Perhaps we are all angels in some way as we help each other. A kind word at the right time can change everything. I was able to go back to my mother with a deeper compassion and to be stronger for my father and sister when they needed that strength.

I will never know who that woman was but I do know that she came to me at a time when I seemed to be floating between worlds. Her presence helped ground and lift me at the same time. And I knew that I would never feel truly alone again.

Bonnie's Song

Enhancing a life to the music

Pam Bostwick

"SING IT 50 times and I never get it right," I complained to my singing teacher, Bonnie.

I was learning the song, *America the Beautiful*. My hearing loss made it difficult for me to follow the alto harmony. Because of my partial sight, I had to use a magnifying glass to read the words.

"Come on sweetheart! Try singing the line again. I know you can do it." Bonnie squeezed my hand. "I'm glad to remind you of the words until you memorize them."

Her encouragement gave me the confidence I needed.

I squared my shoulders. "I want to work hard to sing well, like you."

It took hours going over the song, but Bonnie's patience and my persistence paid off. I finally sang it on my own. Bonnie grabbed me and danced around the room, calling, "You did it." I grinned.

"You are the best teacher ever," I said, and then paused. "I did do a good job, didn't I?"

"You sure did," she said. She hugged me. "I'm proud of you." Bonnie valued and accepted me. I learned many songs after that because she believed in me.

Then one day she broke the news to me. She said with emotion, "I'm sorry, Pam, I have to move."

My stomach lurched with that sinking feeling. I cried a long time in her arms.

The last time I saw Bonnie we shared a special lunch, and chatted and laughed quietly. We both dreaded parting.

Finally, Bonnie walked out on the porch with her arm around me. My mom drove up and waited in the car while Bonnie and I clung to each other. I fought to keep from weeping as she whispered, "You've been like the daughter I never had." She had been that mom for me, too, yet I couldn't tell her. The lump in my throat was so big. Bonnie kissed my cheek.

"I'll miss you."

The horn blared behind me. For a fleeting moment, I wondered if Mom wished we were close like Bonnie and I had been. I couldn't remember the last time my mom had kissed me. I didn't let this thought shatter the precious moment between Bonnie and me.

Bonnie lifted my face to hers. "I don't like goodbyes," she said. "You'll forever be in my heart. Always think of me when you hear our favorite song."

I tossed my head back as we spontaneously broke into our parts. "Oh, beautiful for spacious skies..."

Our voices flowed and I wondered, "How come in this free country I don't have a choice about my friend leaving me?"

I dragged my feet to the car and slowly climbed in. Tears blurred my eyes. Even if I could have seen enough to look back at Bonnie, I wouldn't have done so because it hurt too much.

While we sat in the car, Mom said, "You're a big girl now. You can be tough about this. She's just a music teacher. We can find another one."

I bit back a retort because Mom didn't understand.

The smile in Bonnie's voice made me feel warm all over again. Mom wasn't going to take that joy away from me. I took in a deep breath and said carefully, "I appreciate you wanting to find another teacher for me, but nobody can be my friend, Bonnie."

"Bonnie's an old lady, like me," my mom replied. "How can she be your friend?"

Suddenly, it dawned on me that maybe my mom would like to be my friend, too. Relating to her was like building a bridge across the Grand Canyon. How could I do the impossible?

Thinking of Bonnie's lingering embrace, I thought of a way to build that bridge. With hope I said, "Mom, thanks for giving me the opportunity to take singing lessons. Can I give you a hug?" Mom hesitated, and then replied, "Well, sure I guess." Although it was a tentative hug on both our parts, it was a start.

Bonnie never gave up on me so I wouldn't give up on my mom. With this new challenge of trying to get along with her, I wouldn't miss Bonnie as much.

It's amazing that only seven months with Bonnie at age 11 still has an impact on my life as an adult. Bonnie's devotion and our song will live on in me. To this day, I can't always sing on key but, thanks to Bonnie, I sing even if my efforts are a joyful noise.

Years later, I have the memory of her music, companionship and love. Bonnie filled an empty place in my heart. Now I am free to give my children and grandchildren an outpouring of tenderness.

Bonnie has long since gone home. Each Fourth of July, when *America the Beautiful* is sung, I feel Bonnie near, her rich glorious voice singing the high notes. On earth Bonnie sang like the birds. Now she sings with the angels in Heaven.

Hope Crusader

When you give help, you give hope

Joseph Civitella

H IS NAME WAS Mr. George Hope, and his official title
was principal of St. Francis High School. But everybody affectionately knew him as the "Hope Crusader"
because he never gave up on any of his students, no matter
how much trouble they got into or how many courses they
failed. His favorite saying was, "When you give help, you give
hope." Well, the Hope Crusader gave everyone his help, and
every student had the hope of becoming a "somebody" in life.

One of my buddies, Stanley, was more in a hurry than the
rest of us to become a "somebody." Stan loved to play guitar,
and he was pretty good at it. He even wrote his own songs.
Somehow he hooked up with a bunch of guys a few years older
than him, and they formed a rock band. At the tender age
of 16, he was already playing in bars and nightclubs until all
hours of the night, so you could image that Stan wasn't really
in any shape to attend classes the next day. Even when he did
manage to drag himself to school, he typically fell asleep in
the back row somewhere and hardly ever paid attention to the
teachers.

We all liked Stan, and we all thought he was very cool

playing in a band, but we also saw changes in him that scared many of us. For one thing, he grew his hair long and hardly ever washed it anymore. It was part of his band's image, he said. But he also starting drinking and doing drugs, all part of the "scene," he told us.

None of the teachers was too pleased with Stan as the school year wore on, and even Mr. Hope didn't seem to have a positive influence on him anymore. I clearly remember a parent-teacher night when my parents came home and hugged me, only to tell me that they saw Stan's parents crying in the school hallway. I could only imagine what the teachers had to say about Stan.

It shouldn't have come as a surprise to any of us when a few months later Stan dropped out of school altogether and went on the road with his band. Word had it that a record company was ready to give them a recording contract, but they had to prove themselves as a live act on the road first. We never really heard from Stan again, even though we all expected to hear his band on the radio someday soon. That day never came.

In my final year of high school, I got to know Mr. Hope a little better when I was elected president of the student body. We talked many times about how we might be able to improve some of the after-school intramural activities as well as our sports program. I remember that Mr. Hope also kept talking about creating a music program, and maybe even starting up a marching band if there were enough students interested. When I asked him why he thought a music program was important, he said that maybe there were a few more students out there like Stan who needed to express themselves through music, and if that was the case, then he wanted to help them do it. So typical of our Hope Crusader.

Imagine my surprise when I learned that Mr. Hope had kept in touch with Stan over the two years since he had dropped out. The rock band didn't do as well as originally thought, and Stan apparently was practically on the street without a place to live or any money. Not only had he dropped out of school, but his parents had also kicked him out of their house. I could tell that Mr. Hope regretted he wasn't able to do more for Stan, and I remember thinking that if anybody could help him now, it would be Mr. Hope.

The year after I graduated from high school, I moved out of town to start my collegial studies, and pretty well lost touch with most of my buddies, except Veronica, my high school sweetheart, who attended a nearby college. We both studied health sciences, and I set myself a goal to become a clinical psychologist while Veronica wanted to become a medical doctor. Our studies required a lot from us, but we managed to keep seeing each other at least once a week. We exchanged news from back home whenever something interesting happened, and on one such occasion we both smiled knowingly when a letter from my parents revealed that St. Francis High School was implementing an adult learners program. Any adult who hadn't completed high school would be able to attend evening classes with other adults and obtain their high school graduation certificate. We both wondered if Mr. Hope thought of Stan as his inspiration for that new program.

Veronica and I were lucky to then attend the same university, and many years later we graduated in our respective fields.

We moved back home, and both started working, me as a clinical psychologist and Veronica as a surgeon. Things were going very well for us. Then one day Veronica came home with an amazing story. A new anesthesiologist had been hired at the hospital. She wondered if I could ever guess who it was. I never would have guessed. It was Stan! Somehow Mr. Hope had convinced him to take night courses and to get his high school equivalency. Stan never looked back. And here he was, apparently clean cut, professional in his manner, and ready to be of service in a medical team.

But the most amazing aspect of this whole story doesn't end there. Veronica paged me at my office on a Thursday afternoon to quickly tell me that she was called in to emergency surgery and would not be home at the hour we had agreed to meet. It was part of her profession and I understood perfectly. When she did come home late that evening, she looked tired and somewhat sad. I immediately thought that the surgery did not go as well as she would have liked. That was probably the toughest aspect of her work. But I was mistaken. It wasn't that at all.

Apparently, the patient who came in for emergency surgery was involved in a nasty car accident, and was suffering from severe internal bleeding. Something had to be done immediately or he would not make it past the next hour. To Veronica's utter surprise, she read the patient's name on the chart – Mr. George Hope. He was unconscious, and therefore had no idea who she was. Then she saw Stan looking at the patient, a look of shock in his eyes. She said she asked him if he wanted to be relieved of his duties, and all he did was shake his head.

Veronica smiled now as she concluded her story. During the entire surgery, Stan kept repeating the same phrase under his breath – "When you give help, you give hope." Our Hope Crusader had taught us well, she said, and now it was his turn to receive. The surgery proceeded without a hitch, and another life had been saved. Indeed, when you give help, you give hope.

Surfing for Love in all the Right Places
The virtue of patience

Ellen Gerst

I WAS A YOUNG widow of six years when I decided to look for love again. To be technically correct, I decided to surf for love in all the right ways via the modern-day matchmaker, match.com.

The moment I posted my profile with the dating Internet site, a whole new world opened up to me. I had met my first husband when I was 15 years old. Having married at 20, he was my one and only boyfriend. I did not begin to date until almost three years after his passing. I went on one blind date and ended up becoming engaged to that gentleman. Although he was a nice man and played a huge part in my personal growth, he turned out not to be the right one. So, never having really dated, I decided NOW was the time. I looked upon it as an adventure.

My adventure included talking to and meeting many different men, most of whom I never would have encountered if not for the Internet. I had my favorite places to meet— one for just coffee; one for lunch; and one for drinks and/or dinner. There were days that I frequented these places more than once, and I always wondered if the wait staff thought of me as a "working girl" who showed up with a different man every day! This thought kept a secret smile on my face during the entire date.

Almost a year after I had started Internet dating, the frenetic pace became tiresome. I told the universe that I was glad for all my experiences but that I was now ready for "the one" to find me. I positioned my antennae to stand at full alert and adjusted my eyes and heart to the wide angle and open position. I knew "he" was coming; I just didn't know in what package he would arrive. Consequently, I wanted to remain open to all possibilities.

No more than a few weeks later, a gentleman contacted me and, because I wasn't overly impressed by his profile, I answered his query with an attitude of nonchalance. I *did* have a "wish list" for a mate, and he barely made the cut. He was geographically undesirable, as he lived quite a long distance from me. I also hesitated about him because I normally liked to meet men who were more highly educated, although it turned out he was near genius.

I usually e-mailed men for a bit before moving on to phone conversation, but I simply wasn't engaged by what he said and couldn't think of a thing I wanted to write to him—a rare occurrence for me because I am a great pen pal! Consequently, I decided to go straight to the phone. Again, I strayed from my normal protocol where I gave myself more than enough time to have an initial conversation. However, because I didn't feel a connection to him, I only allotted him 15 minutes. I did enjoy the brief conversation more than I thought I would but had to end it abruptly because I was off to a meeting. He was going out of town and said he would call me upon his return. I had heard that line once or twice before so I was not holding my breath waiting for his call. Matter of fact, I was meeting three or four other guys in the interim.

Anyway, he did call me—and it was actually four days earlier than he said he would. I happened to be trying out for a game show near where he lived so, as long as I was on his side of town, we decided to meet for coffee afterwards. I was to call him when I was done. When I did call at the appointed time, he neither answered his home phone nor his cell phone. To top it off, his voice mail was full so I couldn't leave a message. This did not bode well. I started to drive home, but I continued to try his cell phone until I was almost out of the area.

Eventually, he picked up and apologized profusely. He had been out of range and the calls were not going through. We mutually decided to still meet. I would wait until he could drive to where I was. So, there I was on a Saturday night waiting for a half hour in the dark parking lot of a Starbucks for a guy I wasn't even sure I wanted to meet.

He finally arrived, and I stepped out of my car to greet him. Not disappointing, but I didn't think he looked much like his picture. He came toward me, and I was prepared to shake his hand. He decided he would rather give me a big hug. Again, not an auspicious beginning from my point of view; it overstepped my boundaries to hug someone I had never met before or to whom I had barely spoken. After that initial awkwardness, we ended up talking for two hours, and it was an enjoyable conversation; however, I did not hear any bells or whistles or see flashing lights. During the course of the conversation, he asked me out for the following week. I agreed, but kept in mind that I had also heard this line before and would believe it when I heard from him again.

Of course, he did call, and we did go out. We had a wonderful time full of laughter and good cheer. We continued to see each other, talk on the phone, and e-mail each other quite often. Each time I saw him, he became more and more attractive to me until I thought him the most adorable, sweetest, nicest man I had ever met. Over the next couple of months, we forged a relationship built on mutual values, respect and admiration. Since we both were more than willing to reveal our innermost thoughts and let the other see inside of us, emotional intimacy was easy and quick to reach. I came to truly believe that this was "the one" for whom I was waiting.

Now, this may seem like just a sweet story of true love winning in the end, but unbeknownst to me, I was the recipient of my future husband's "thin thread" moment.

Weeks after we started dating, he confided in me that he had seen my profile almost a year before. Being quite intuitive, as he read my profile and stared at my picture, he knew that I was his "one." He also knew that I wasn't quite ready to meet him. How right he was! I was just starting my dating adventure at that time and I would not have recognized him if he had showed up earlier. He told me that he checked my profile often to determine if he thought I was ready. Finally, like a lightning bolt, he knew it was time to connect. When he saw me in the parking lot for the first time, our entire future life together flashed before his eyes. He felt as if he already knew me, and, of course, moved to hug me rather than shake my hand. And, as the saying goes, the rest is history. We have just celebrated seven happy years of marriage.

Believe in Yourself

Actualizing my dreams

Mary Jones

This story was originally published in The Power of Persistence *by Justin Sachs, Fall 2009. It is reprinted here with permission.*

WHEN I WAS 38 years old, my husband Jim died of a sudden massive heart attack. He had just turned 40, was a high school and college athlete who continued to exercise throughout the years, and was in good physical shape.

I owned a corporate recruiting firm at the time. Years later, as I approached my 50th birthday, I began to think seriously about getting into radio. Prior to recruiting, I was director of a nonprofit organization, and during those years had recorded public service announcements. I always enjoyed being in the studio and even then thought about pursuing a radio career at some point.

Having always been a goal-oriented person and giving significance to life's milestones, my upcoming 50th birthday was looming large. While I still enjoyed my recruiting business, I longed for the feeling of exhilaration and daily challenge that had faded over the years.

So, a goal was set. It was the end of 2000, and my 50th

would be in November of the next year. I told myself that I would in fact have a talk show by my next birthday.

There were no more than a handful of local talk shows in the Hartford, Connecticut area at the time and I had no connections or contacts within that industry. But what I did have was determination and commitment. After all, I had set a goal, and the clock was ticking.

I soon realized that I had something else, too. Something that was fueled by my husband's death and that was providing me great encouragement and drive.

I realized that Jim hadn't had a chance to fulfill his dreams, to realize all that he could have been and done in his life. But I did. And, at that moment, I decided not only to go after my dream with enormous gusto, but to do it for him. I made a commitment to myself to take full advantage of my life and to make the most of having the opportunity to do so.

I was able to secure a meeting with the general manager of a radio station. I pitched my idea of a show on careers—a natural outflow of my recruiting business. I pointed out that there wasn't a program on that topic in the local market, why there should be one, and why I should be the person to host it. He was receptive to the idea and asked me to put together a demo tape.

I learned along the way—about mid-year 2001—that the radio industry is like any other industry. It's driven by sales, and sales equates to advertising in radio. So, while figuring out and working on my demo, I discovered that I would also need to bring several advertisers to my show.

As with many things in life, and most goals, when surprises

arise that make the process more difficult than initially thought, it's easy to abandon your aspirations. Then, and mostly then, you need to hold onto that which gives you that inner belief in yourself, and the resolve to continue on. It's about persistence.

For me, that persistence reappeared each time I reminded myself of my commitment to make the absolute most of my life—at least I had the opportunity to do so. Each reminder brought me a renewed sense of energy and excitement about moving forward. Working through and moving past the obstacles then became a fun challenge. Attitude truly makes the difference.

I completed my demo, submitted it and waited for "the call." That call would tell me I could start my show. I had also secured a couple of advertisers. My 50th birthday was just a week away.

I decided to follow up with the station's general manager and placed a call to him three days before my birthday. No callback by my birthday. But two days later I heard back—my show would start shortly after the first of the year.

I have now been doing my show for eight years and have loved every moment. After the first year, I switched from focusing on careers to talking about issues of everyday life from a positive perspective.

The need for me to bring in advertisers continued until the show became established and popular. At that point, the station committed its sales staff to selling my show.

One of the things that always has been important to me— even as a young woman—is not to have regrets at the end of my life. There have been a multitude of surveys over the years asking elderly people to reflect back on their lives in an attempt to capture some of their acquired wisdom. Invariably, the responses touch upon regretting not what they did, but what they did not do. My husband's death reinforced that and continues to remind and motivate me.

However, I've learned along the way that while some people have that drive and determination to follow their dreams, goals and aspirations, it can be fleeting. Wanting something badly is very different than actually making it happen.

That difference, while critical, is also simple. It's being willing to persist.

What has worked for me is to figure out why each dream and goal is important, and what is driving me to fulfill it. More than the goal itself, it's about the motivation for wanting it. For me, it is clear. I want to experience as much as life has to offer, before the time comes when I no longer can. That drive in and of itself gives me the persistence to pursue with vigor those things that I set my sights on.

That drive is different for everyone. And it will vary from time to time, goal to goal. But before you decide to enlist your time, energy and resources into any pursuit, think about why it's important to you. If the reason isn't one of significance or emotional value, reconsider. Only that will propel you to overcome the obstacles you'll undoubtedly meet along the way. Only that will feed your determination. Dream your dreams, understand your motivations, live life to the fullest and persist until you achieve all you desire.

A Message from Anne Witkavitch

We receive many "thin thread" stories and spend countless hours reading each one. We are in awe of the beautiful writing and how each story inspires us in its own special way. Deciding which to choose is always a difficult task.

The stories in this anthology celebrate the diverse ways each of us connects with each other in life and, more importantly, the ways those connections make us a more complete part of this universe. Each "thin thread" is an opportunity to learn, grow, share and find hope.

We want to thank everyone kind enough to share their stories with us, and particularly those whose words you read within these pages.

Anne Witkavitch,
Managing Editor

Thanks to our
Thin Threads Contributors

Tom Adessa is a lifelong resident of the beautiful Finger Lakes Region of New York State. He is a former animal cruelty investigator and steelworker. Although not pursuing writing until 2007, he is a contributing writer for the Syracuse Post Standard. Additionally he has self-published a children's book, *Butternuts for Rexford*, a charming story set in the Adirondack Mountains that teaches children the value of friendships and the power of courage. Tom can be contacted at para454@roadrunner.com

Tracy Austin is originally from Victoria, Texas. She returned to college to complete her bachelor's degree in communication at the University of Texas of the Permian Basin at age 39. Until then, she worked in support roles, mostly in medical and dental offices. She didn't discover her passion for writing until her mid-40s, so she identifies herself as a "late-bloomer." Tracy currently lives in Odessa, Texas, with her life-partner and their feline fur-babies.

Francine L. Baldwin-Billingslea is a mother, a grandmother, a breast cancer survivor and a second-time-around newlywed who has recently found a passion for writing. She has been published in *Rambler* magazine and in several anthologies, including *Chicken Soup for the Soul, Whispering Angel* books and Lachance Publishing, to name a few. She has also written an inspirational memoir titled, *Through It All*, which can be purchased on www.Xlibris.com, www.barnesandnoble.com and www.Amazon.com. Some of the proceeds are donated to breast cancer research.

Denise Bar-Aharon is the co-founder and president of Make-A-Wish Israel, which was established in 1996 in honor of her brother, David Spero. Today she also serves on the board of Make-A-Wish International. Denise is president of B.T.C. International, a buying and sourcing agency in Israel representing top American and Canadian firms. She received a B.S. in international marketing from the Fashion Institute of Technology in New York, where she serves on the International Trade and Marketing Advisory Board of Directors. Denise is a sculptor and was commissioned to make a public sculpture in Israel in 2001. The sculpture was inspired by Make-A-Wish and dedicated to her brother. She resides in Israel, is married to Avi her life partner, and has three beautiful children.

Pam Bostwick's many articles appear in magazines, newspapers and anthologies, including several in *Chicken Soup for the Soul*. She is legally blind and hearing-impaired and enjoys life. She loves her country home, the beach and playing guitar, and is a volunteer counselor. She has seven children and 11 grandchildren. She happily remarried on July 7, 2007. Email her at pamloves7@verizon.net.

Cathy Brown lives in Indianapolis, Ind., with her husband, son, daughter, Rottweiler, and a perpetual slumber party of teenagers. She is passionate about teaching and mentoring the next generation to recognize and chase their God-given potential; and she applies this passion in an international mentorship program and online private franchising business. Additionally, Cathy is a freelance writer and Christian event planner, and insists that the ideal workplace includes turquoise water, white sand, blue skies, seagulls and – of course – teenagers.

Virginia Cassarino-Brown lives on the rocky coast of Harpswell, Maine, where she takes advantage of all her home state has to offer! She spends her free time writing essays, memoirs and children's stories and is actively engaged in turning her front yard into an edible garden! Some of her work has been published in the magazine *Adventures for the Average Woman* and she is actively in the process of publishing her first children's book, *Tangled Loon*, which was inspired by real-life events.

Kathe Campbell lives her dream on a Montana mountain with her mammoth donkeys, a Keeshond and a few kitties. Three children, 11 grands and three greats round out her herd. She is a prolific writer on Alzheimer's, and her stories are found on many ezines. Kathe is a contributing author to the *Chicken Soup For The Soul* and *Cup of Comfort* series, numerous anthologies, RX for Writers, magazines and medical journals. Her email address is kathe@wildblue.net.

June Can is an author, artist, psychic healer and channel. She is a lifelong student of the healing arts, and has taught shiatsu, qigong and dance, and is a master reiki practitioner. She holds a bachelor's degree in English literature, musicology and dance, and a master's degree in information and library science. Her book *Healing Relationships, Healing the World: A New Formula for World Peace* was published in 2009. She also performs and choreographs with the Clark Dance Theater. Her website is http://junecanchannel.blogspot.com/.

Elynne Chaplik-Aleskow, founding general manager of WYCC-TV/PBS and distinguished professor emeritus of Wright College in Chicago, is an author, public speaker, adult storyteller and award-winning educator and broadcaster. Her nonfiction stories and essays have been published in numerous anthologies such as *Chicken Soup for the Soul* and NPR's *This I Believe* and various magazines including the international *Jerusalem Post Magazine*. Elynne is married to her best friend, Richard Noel Aleskow. Her website is http://LookAroundMe.blogspot.com.

Kitty Chappell, international speaker/award-winning author, has authored two books, including numerous articles and poetry. Her first book, *I Can Forgive If I Want To* (Vocatio Publishers) now in five languages, was originally released as *Sins of a Father, Forgiving the Unforgivable*. Her second, *Good Mews, Inspurrational Stories for Cat-Lovers,* contains true stories about her cats. Kitty has appeared on radio and television in the United States and Poland. Kitty lives in Chandler, Ariz., with her cat, Miss Middy. Her website is www.kittychappell.com.

Joseph Civitella, Msc.D., writer and line editor for *Thin Thread Stories*, is a lifelong student of spiritual metaphysics – the quest for truth, meaning and purpose. Along with his Ph.D. in metaphysical sciences, Joseph is also an ordained minister. His writing credits include the novel *Shadows of Tomorrow*, a compilation of poems and prose called *The Blossoming* and a CD of original songs, *Soulace*. He operates the School of LifeWork, based on his nonfiction book *Turning your Passion into a Profession*. Additional information on Joseph can be found at:
-Joseph@SchoolofLifeWork.com
-www.SchoolofLifeWork.com
-www.MySpace.com/SchoolofLifeWork

Joan Clayton says that writing has always been her passion. Having three energetic boys and 31 years of teaching first- and second-graders, she had a lot to write about. Since she retired, writing has taken priority. Her ex-students have nominated her twice in *Who's Who Among America's Teachers* and she feels blessed to meet them somewhere all grown up. She gets many hugs, and their love notes are kept in her treasure book and her heart.

Lorri B. Danzig MS, CSL, holds a master's in Jewish studies with a focus on aging, death and dying. A Certified Sage-ing® Leader and president of Let It Shine Journeys, she teaches programs focused on the spiritual tasks of life-completion — harvesting wisdom, creating a legacy, mentoring and forgiveness work. Lorri writes poetry and creative nonfiction. She is now at work on a memoir exploring a year of recovery and growth.

Michele Rae Eich taught middle school students for 18 years before leaving the job she loved to pursue a career as a freelance writer and public speaker. She is the founder of Finally Free Ministry and author of the book *Wolf Boy: A Case of Mistaken Identity.* Michele and her husband, Lynn have six wonderful and energetic children. They enjoy gardening, canning, traveling and attending their kids' activities. Michele is currently working on her second book, *The Garden Restored.*

Terri Elders, LCSW, lives near Colville, Wash., where she walks two protective dogs, cuddles three narcissistic cats, raises zillions of zinnias and writes narrative essays. Her work has appeared in dozens of anthologies and magazines, including *Chicken Soup for the Soul, A Cup of Comfort and the HCI Ultimate, Patchwork Path,* and *Literary Cottage Hero* series. She blogs at http://atouchoftarragon.blogspot.com/ and can be befriended on Facebook. Contact her: telders@hotmail.com. She's a public member of the Washington State Medical Commission.

James Fox,"Foxtale," is a husband, father, former Scoutmaster and currently a volunteer canoe guide for the state parks system. He still works for food, but his experiences in the mountains and along the streams and rivers of California are often the basis for his short stories and poems. Usually writing in the creative nonfiction genre, he has recently delved into fiction. Eleven of Jim's short-short stories have been published in various periodicals. His haiku, *wings,* was published and later chosen to introduce "The Written Word" exhibits at the 2005 Lodi Sandhill Crane Festival. His one lament is that the late Andy Warhol promised us all a few minutes of fame; fortune would have been better.

Sandra Freeman, a lifelong lover of music, started playing the piano at five years old, and, at that tender age, she was able to listen to a piece of music and play it by ear. She went on to hone her craft by studying music performance at Juilliard and the State University of New York at New Paltz. Sandra has worked as a music recreational therapist and executive assistant and is now a youth volunteer. Always an animal lover, she is currently writing *Are You Ready To Be a Pet Owner?* You can connect with her at sandtone@aol.com

Ellen Gerst, a grief and relationship coach, writer and speaker, pursues her passion for lifelong learning and assisting others in reaching their goals in Phoenix, Arizona. Her writing credits include *A Practical Guide to Widow/erhood and Love After Loss: Writing the Rest of Your Story,* both born from her own experience as a young widow who emerged from mourning with renewed energy and a zest for living. She delights her clients, readers and audiences with her heartfelt passion and unique ability to see endless new solutions, possibilities and opportunities.

Howard Gleichenhaus was born in Philadelphia in 1943, and grew up in the Bronx, N.Y. He holds a bachelor's degree in biology from Southern Connecticut State University and a pair of master's degrees from Fairleigh Dickinson University; one in biology and a second in psychology. After a short career in biochemistry research, Howard taught high school biology for 35 years in the Clarkstown Central School District, Rockland County, New York. During that time he also operated his own portrait/wedding/bar mitzvah photography business. Now retired, Howard and his wife, Fredda, live in Delray Beach, Fla. They have two married sons, Corey and Rob, as well as two grandchildren who live in nearby Boynton Beach.

Harriet Hodgson has been an independent journalist for 30-plus years. Her writing comes from experience and Hodgson has shared her experiences on more then 160 talk shows, including CBS Radio and dozens of television stations, including CNN. She is the author of 27 books, including *Writing to Recover: The Journey from Loss and Grief to a New Life*. Her work is cited in *Who's Who of American Women, Who's Who in America* and other directories. See www.harriethodgson.com for more information.

Erika Hoffman has been submitting writings for four years, and she has been fortunate to have 60 pieces published. Most are nonfiction narratives that found homes in national anthologies such as A *Cup of Comfort, Chicken Soup for the Soul* and *Patchwork Path*. Erika grew up in New Jersey, attending schools in Plainfield and Scotch Plains before college at Duke University. She taught seventh-grade language arts in East Brunswick, N.J.; high school English and French in Atlanta; Ga., and several different grades and subjects in Siler City, N.C.

Mary Johnson has two daughters ages 14 and 16. She lives in Los Angeles and works at a local university. Her careers throughout her life have been various, including being a legal secretary, paralegal, full-time mom and laboratory tech. If you are reading this story and your father is still alive, she says, "You are lucky. Spend some time with him for no particular reason at all and tell him that you love him."

Mary Jones is the host of *The Mary Jones Show* on WDRC-AM in Hartford and its three affiliate Connecticut stations. She also does a weekly segment, *All That and More,* on NBC Connecticut. Mary is co-author of *Incredible Life* and a contributing writer of *The Power of Persistence,* which reached #1 on Amazon's self-improvement category. Mary's show has evolved into a strong community of listeners who share conversation and insights into issues of daily life. Her overall theme and message is Believe in Yourself! She lives with her wonderful husband and equally wonderful West Highland White Terrier, Archie.

Nancy Julien-Kopp grew up in Chicago but has lived in the Flint Hills of Kansas for many years. She and her retired husband enjoy traveling, attending Kansas State football and basketball games, and family gatherings. Although she started writing late in life, Nancy has been published in nine *Chicken Soup for the Soul* books, several other anthologies, ezines, newspapers and magazines. Once a classroom teacher, she now teaches through the written word. Her website is www.writergrannysworld.blogpsot.com.

Madeleine Kuderick is passionate about writing stories that touch the heart. Her work appears in *Chicken Soup for the Soul, Cup of Comfort* and other anthologies. She is a member of the Society of Children's Book Writers and Illustrators, and a graduate of the Institute of Children's Literature. She holds a master's degree from Saint Leo University. Madeleine lives on Florida's Gulf Coast with her husband and two children. She hopes that everybody has a Frosty in their life. Her website is www.madeleinekuderick.com.

Ruth Lambert was the founder and CEO of Forms & Worms, which sold books and forms to 36,000 appraisers for 22 years until 1998. Her husband, Henry S. Harrison, has 28 appraisal books in print. Ruth self-published two other books: *101 Survival Tactics for New and Used Parents* and *The Houses Cookbook*, based on American house styles. Ruth has four children and 4.5 grandkids. She loves gardening, reading, writing, tennis, walking, crocheting and entertaining at her summerhouse in Branford, Conn.

John J. Lesjack and Carol Lee, both retired school teachers, live in northern California. John has been published in the *San Francisco Chronicle Sunday Magazine, The Ultimate Teacher, Chicken Soup for the Soul – Father/Son; Chocolate Lover; Living Faith; Grit, Whispers from Heaven, The Ultimate Mom* and other national publications. Responses to this story may be sent to Jlesjack@gmail.com.

Gary Luerding is a retired army NCO and high school attendance officer. He and his wife, Lynne, live in southern Oregon and have been married for 47 years. They have three children, eight grandchildren and one great-granddaughter. Gary enjoys writing and has been published in several magazines and numerous anthologies such as *Chicken Soup for the Soul* and *Cup of Comfort*. He can be reached at garyluer@frontiernet.net.

Dean FH Macy, D.Litt., began his writing career at 26 when he ghostwrote several sci-fi stories for now famous authors. His genres include fantasy and science fiction, young adult fiction and screenplays. He is currently working on his humorous and often poignant book, *Treasures In My Attic*, about his adventures raising 19 children.

Kathy McAfee is a foster/adoptive parent, professional speaker, author and executive presentation coach. Known as "America's Marketing Motivator," her mission is to help business leaders and career professionals leverage more of their energy, knowledge and relationships to create positive changes in the world. A black belt in tae kwon do, Kathy teaches women's self-defense workshops to help empower women and girls. Kathy resides in Simsbury, Conn., with her husband and two adopted sons. Learn more about Kathy at her web site, www. MarketingMotivator.net.

Milda Misevicius is the executive vice president of Korey Kay & Partners, a New York City-based creative advertising agency. Along with producing major award-winning advertising campaigns, Milda has been in front of the camera as well as behind it. She has written and produced a documentary; written a series of short plays to help cancer survivors and their families; written four original screenplays and created a children's history book series. Currently, Milda is putting the finishing touches on a novel.

Linda O'Connell, a distinguished member of the St. Louis Writer's Guild, is an early-childhood teacher and an accomplished writer. Linda, a positive thinker, writes from the heart, bares her soul and finds humor in everyday situations. Although she has won awards for poetry and fiction, she considers herself an essayist. Her stories appear in a dozen *Chicken Soup for the Soul* books, *Voices of Autism, Reminisce* magazine, *Sasee* magazine and numerous anthologies and literary magazines. Linda blogs at http://lindaoconnell.blogspot.com.

Lucien Padawer, born in Brussels, Belgium, immigrated with his family to the USA in 1942 after escaping German occupation. A New York University graduate, Lucien was the first trench coat importer of fashion from Europe after WWII. He subsequently opened the first import boutique on Fifth Avenue (Parisette) in 1952. He also distributed imports from the family fashion business (Import Associates Stores) to 70 start-up retailers including Casual Corner and Ann Taylor. By 1959, the members had grown to many hundreds of stores and as the association was no longer manageable he started Foxrun. By the end of the millennium, it became the leading fashion outerwear company in the USA.

Perry P. Perkins, novelist, blogger, and award-winning travel writer, is a stay-at-home dad who lives with his wife, Victoria, and their three-year-old daughter, Grace, in the Pacific Northwest. Perry has written for hundreds of magazines, and his inspirational stories have been included in 12 *Chicken Soup for the Soul* anthologies as well. His books include the novels *Just Past Oysterville, Shoalwater Voices, Elk Hunters Don't Cry* and his new short-story collection, *Four From Left Field.* More of Perry's work can be found at www.perryperkinsbooks.com.

Becky Povich lives near St. Louis, Mo. She didn't begin writing until she was in her late 40s. That's when she realized it was her true passion. Since then she's had stories published in several anthologies and literary journals. She also wrote a weekly newspaper column for two years, from which she is on hiatus while working on her first book, a memoir titled *That Crowbar Changed Everything!* You can reach Becky through her blog, www.beckypovich.blogspot.com.

Kathryn Rothschadl is an aspiring freelance writer from Waukesha, Wis. She has a husband and two children. She has a background in graphic design as well as newspaper journalism. In her spare time, she loves to read, scrapbook and spend time with family and friends.

Joyce M. Saltman is a professor emerita of special education at Southern Connecticut State University, and has been a motivational speaker on the subject of "Laughter: Rx for Survival" since 1983. Known as "the guru of laughter," she has informed and entertained thousands of organizations in the United States and abroad, as far as Osaka, Japan, and Sydney, Australia. She received her doctorate at Columbia University because she loved the color of its doctoral gown! Joyce has two children, Steven Anisman, MD, and Beth Anisman-Berzofsky, JD, and a stepson, Mark Saltman. All are married to wonderful people!

Kelly Seymour lived for three years in Japan, where she taught English in public schools in Kawasaki and Tokyo. She recently completed a novel set in Japan; her work has appeared in *The Southern Review, Massachusetts Review, Gettysburg Review,* and other magazines. Find her online at Crazy Pete's Blotter: http://www.thecrazypetesblotter.blogspot.com/.

Carol Sharpe's life has been a very busy one with four children as well as a 15-yearold foster daughter. Her positions included cosmetic manager for 30 years. Carol decided to leave and enter nursing with seniors. It was always something she wanted to do. When she retired, she went into writing. At this stage, she has 12 grandchildren and three great-grandchildren. Carol still plans on writing now and in the future. It's her passion!

Sylvia Skrmetta lives on the Mississippi Gulf Coast with her husband of 42 years. She is the author of her mother's memoirs, *Giovanna: Angels in Hell*, which is available online at Amazon and Barnes and Noble. Sylvia has won two short story contests and has written several articles for various local magazines and newspapers. She is also a semi-retired registered nurse, artist, grandmother and full-time dreamer.

Dorothy Stephens is a former teacher and freelance writer whose work has appeared in the *New York Times, Miami Herald, Los Angeles Times, Adventure Cyclist, The World and I, the Larcom Review* and other national publications. She co-authored the book *Discovering Marblehead* and was a finalist in the 1997 Bread Loaf Bakeless Creative Nonfiction competition. She and her husband live in Marblehead, Mass.

Deborah Straw is a writer and educator who lives in northern Vermont with her husband, a mixed-breed dog and two Maine coon cats. Her first book, *Natural Wonders of the Florida Keys,* was published in August 1999 by Country Roads Press/NTC

Contemporary Publishing. Her second is *The Healthy Pet Manual, A Guide to the Prevention and Treatment of Cancer* (2005, second edition). Widely published as a journalist, book reviewer and essayist, she has written for many magazines, and her work has been included in several anthologies.

Joyce E. Sudbeck is retired and resides near St. Louis with her husband of 56 years. Being fairly new to the writing world, she is grateful to have had her work published in *Chicken Soup for the Soul books, Liguorian* magazine, *Good Old Days* magazine, and now *Thin Threads*. She placed first in local poetry contests (2009 and 2010). Her hobbies include cooking, knitting, crocheting, choir, piano and painting. Of course, her favorite hobby is writing.

Annmarie Tait resides in Conshohocken, Pa., with her husband, Joe, and Sammy the Yorkie. In addition to writing stories about her large Irish Catholic family, Annmarie also has a passion for cooking and crocheting. In her spare time, she likes to sing and record Irish and American folk songs. Annmarie has stories published in several *Chicken Soup for the Soul* volumes as well as the *Patchwork Path* series. You may contact Annmarie at irishbloom@aol.com.

Lucy Parker Watkins has spent the last several years seeking wisdom from her own life-altering experiences. As a feature writer for a regional women's publication, she began finding spiritual answers while interviewing successful women in her community who, like herself, had overcome a myriad of challenges. As a result, she made it her personal and professional quest to write her own story along with other true-life stories in the hope of offering readers inspiration and the realization they that are not alone in their challenges.

Jesse White founded the School for Wonder for personal development and creativity in 1987. She has performed throughout the United States as a singer/songwriter, poet, motivational speaker and advocate for social justice. She released two books of contemplative poetry, produced three all-original CDs of her music, and 20 spoken-word artists on her label, Authentic Voicework Records. Jesse was co-editor and publisher of *Manzanita Quarterly Literary Review,* and is currently working on a memoir.

Lee Williams lives in Palm Bay, Fla., with her husband, Allen, and their very needy cat, Judah. Her three grown children are scattered across the States. Along with writing, she is obsessed with history, which makes traveling anywhere (her third love) that much more enjoyable. Lee writes for a women's interest magazine for the Space Coast and her work is endlessly inspired by her Southern roots.

Sheila Williams is a freelance writer living in Los Angeles with her large and lovely pug, Miss Phoebe Rose. Sheila confesses to be an optimistic pessimist and an introverted extrovert. She has been "unduly concerned about the actions of others" since the third grade. Inspirational reading is her passion and to be able to inspire others is her opportunity to express thanks for the kindness of strangers.

Ferida Wolff is author of 17 children's books and three essay books, her latest being the award-winning picture book *The Story Blanket and Missed Perceptions: Challenge Your Thoughts Change Your Thinking.* Her work appears in anthologies, newspapers, magazines, in www.seniorwomen.com and in her nature blog http://feridasbackyard.blogspot.com. Visit her at www.feridawolff.com.

Dallas Woodburn is the author of two collections of short stories and a forthcoming novel; her nonfiction has appeared in *Family Circle, Writer's Digest,* and *The Los Angeles Times.* In 2001, she founded Write On! For Literacy, a nonprofit organization that empowers youth through writing. Most recently, Dallas edited and published *Dancing With The Pen,* an anthology of stories, essays and poems by young writers. Learn more at http://www.writeonbooks.org and http://dallaswoodburn.blogspot.com.

Greg Woodburn is the founder and president of Give Running (www.giverunning.org), a nonprofit organization that shares a love for running and its benefits with disadvantaged youth by collecting, cleaning and donating athletic shoes. Greg's involvement with Give Running has been featured in *Reader's Digest* and *People* magazine, as well as on CNN's *Headline News.* He is a junior at the University of Southern California, where he runs for the track & field team and serves on the Trojan Athletic Senate.

Haiyan Zhang is a certified management consultant whose mission in life is to contribute to and facilitate the success of others through attitude, aptitude and action. Combining Western business disciplines and Eastern philosophies, Haiyan's advice is grounded in insights gained working with senior leaders in a variety of organization and her personal journey living and working in China, the Middle East and North America. Haiyan holds an MBA and MA and makes frequent presentations in English, Chinese and French.

About Stacey K. Battat
Editor-in-Chief

STACEY BATTAT CO-FOUNDED KIWI Publishing with her husband, Eitan, in 2005. She is a speaker and has been inspiring audiences for the past 15 years. She connects with her audiences, and, since her broadcast journalism years in Florida (having graduated from the University of Florida) and Israel, she has captured the passion in many people's life stories. She won a number of story awards from the Cable TV Magazine show, *Hello Jerusalem*.

Stacey and her husband have three children, and currently reside in the Greater New Haven, Connecticut area.

To inquire about inviting Stacey to speak for your association, business or organization, or to purchase more of this edition at a bulk discount, please e-mail info@thinthreads. com or call 1-866-836-7913

More Thin Threads Titles Are Now Available

We are certain that you enjoyed this *Thin Threads* anthology. The Classic Edition is available for $17.95 and contains 50 real stories of life changing moments. Many special edition volumes are also available from Kiwi Publishing. Watch for new books in the series in 2011, or subscribe to the series and stay inspired all year long.

To purchase a copy of any of these titles or to subscribe to the *Thin Threads* Book Series visit www.thinthreads.com.

Customized Thin Threads Books

A card, book and gift... all in one!

www.CustomizeMyBook.com

Your Name Here

-Pick your occasion
-Select your favorite stories
-Choose from 15 different covers
-Personalize inside and outside
   front cover text
-Submit your order!

Your customized *Thin Threads* book will be a keep-sake for years to come!

Visit www.CustomizeMyBook.com to give it a try. You can even find a video tutorial which will walk you through the process.

Please tell us your story!

KIWI PUBLISHING is currently collecting stories for upcoming editions of *Thin Threads*. If you or someone you know has experienced a life changing moment, please tell us your story!

Our contributors are the heart of the *thin threads* mission and an integral part of the *thin threads* legacy. Please check our website (www.thinthreads.com) for additional information and submission guidelines.

SUBMIT ONLINE:
    www.thinthreads.com
SUBMIT BY MAIL:
    KIWI Publishing Inc.
    P.O. Box 3852
    Woodbridge, CT 06525

IPS 101818